Narcissisti
Clinical Perspectives

Edited by

Judy Cooper and Nilda Maxwell

JASON ARONSON INC.
Northvale, New Jersey
London

This book was printed and bound by Book-mart Press
of North Bergen, New Jersey

Copyright © 1995 by Whurr Publishers Ltd.
US Edition 1995–Jason Aronson Inc.

10 9 8 7 6 5 4 3 2 1

Library of Congress Cataloging-in-Publication Data

Narcissistic wounds : clinical perspectives / edited by Judy Cooper
and Nilda Maxwell.
     p.   cm.
  Includes bibliographical references and index
  ISBN 1-56821-747-1 (alk. paper)
  1. Narcississm. I. Cooper, Judy.   II. Maxwell, Nilda.
  [DNLM: 1. Narcissism. 2. Object Attachment. 3. Anxiety,
Separation. 4. Psychoanalytic Therapy.   WM 460.5E3 N2223   1996]
RC553.N36N373   1996
616.85'85—dc20
DNLM/DLM
for Library of Congress   95-35828

Manufactured in the United States of America. Jason Aronson Inc. offers books
and cassettes. For information and catalog write to Jason Aronson Inc., 230
Livingston Street, Northvale, New Jersey 07647.

Contents

Contributors

Judy Cooper
Full Member, British Association of Psychotherapists. Author of: *Speak Of Me As I Am: The Life and Work of Masud Khan.* (London: Karnac Books, 1993).

Hazel Danbury
Full Member, British Association of Psychotherapists. Lecturer in Applied Social Studies at Royal Holloway and Bedford New College, London University.

Sara Flanders, PhD
Member of the British Psycho-Analytical Society. Staff member at Brent Adolescent Centre. Editor of: *The Dream Discourse Today* (London: Routledge, 1993).

Liz Good
Associate Member, Association for Group and Individual Psychotherapy. Consultant, Addiction Unit, Sturt House Psychiatric Clinic. Clinical Supervisor, Addiction Unit, HMP Holloway Prison.

Nilda Maxwell
Psychoanalytic Researcher. Previously researcher at the Argentine Psychoanalytical Society and Visiting Senior Research Fellow at Sussex University.

David Morgan
Associate Member, British Psycho-Analytical Society. Consultant Clinical Psychologist, Portman Clinic.

Maria Pozzi
Child Psychotherapist. Associate Member, British Association of Psychotherapists. Child psychotherapist at Hitchin Child and Family Consultation Clinic. Teaching at the Tavistock Clinic and London Centre for Psychotherapy.

Joan Raphael-Leff
Member, British Psycho-Analytical Society. Member, Steering Committee, Royal Society of Medicine for Maternity and the Newborn. Author of: *Psychological Processes of Childbearing* (London: Chapman & Hall, 1991); *Pregnancy: the Inside Story* (London: Sheldon Press, 1993).

Salomon Resnik, Dr
Full Member Psycho-Analytical International Association. Training Analyst. Author of *Mental Space* (London: Karnac Books, 1995).

Stanley Ruszczynski
Full Member, British Association of Psychotherapists. Senior Marital Psychotherapist at the Tavistock Marital Studies Institute. Editor of: *Psychotherapy With Couples* (London: Karnac Books, 1993). Co-editor of: *Intrusiveness and Intimacy in the Couple.* (London: Karnac Books, 1995).

David Livingstone Smith
Director of the MA in Psychotherapy and Counselling at Regent's College, London. Author of: *Hidden Conversations: An Introduction to Communicative Psychoanalysis* (London: Routledge, 1991).

Daniel Twomey
Associate Member, British Association of Psychotherapists. Previously worked in Child Guidance.

Peter Wilson
Child Psychoanalyst. Director of Young Minds. Previously Senior Clinical Tutor, Institute of Psychiatry, London.

Anne Zachary, Dr
Associate Member, British Psycho-Analytical Society. Consultant psychotherapist in the NHS at the Portman Clinic. Clinic Tutor at the Portman Clinic.

Foreword

As a contribution to this book, I would like to go back to some original versions of the myth of Narcissus and its implications for the concepts of primary and secondary narcissism and narcissistic wounds.

In Ovid's *Metamorphoses*, the major poetic version of the myth, Narcissus is the product of a violent but exciting copulation between two waters. Leiriope, the beautiful nymph, was raped by the river-god Cephisus and gave birth to a beautiful baby boy, Narcissus. Leiriope consulted the seer Teiresias, who predicted that if the boy was ever to know himself he would die. Thus, in order to remain alive, Narcissus had to struggle against his desire to see and to know himself.

One day he met Echo, a beautiful nymph, who found him very attractive. She could no longer use her voice, except to repeat what someone else said. She longed to address Narcissus, but of course was unable to speak first. The arrogant Narcissus showed no response to Echo, who became so unhappy that she spent the rest of her life pining for him, becoming thinner and thinner until she vanished, and only her voice remained.

Narcissus was not interested in other people. From a primary objectless narcissistic view, he showed interest only in himself or in his narcissistic double, male or female (according to Pausanias, he was nostalgic for his female side or twin, who died when he was born). Looked at as a narcissistic object relationship, he was seized by his tremendous curiosity and wanted to re-experience the primal scene to witness his origins as the son of two waters issued from an exciting and violent copulation. Impelled by his voyeuristic and sexual drives, he desired to encounter his original parents in the act of copulating. Indeed, he was fascinated with and hypnotized by this mythical fantasy. He identified with his object by *projective narcissistic identification* to such an extent that he was both himself and his copulating object. Gazing enraptured into the waters, he died by his own hand, plunging a dagger into his breast. His blood soaked the earth, and he became transformed into a beautiful

vii

narcotic flower: the narcissus. This fascinating hypnotic/narcotic Narcissus wanted to be virgin of all otherness – he was himself and his object except in the depths of his inner abyss (bottomless mental space), where he desired to recreate his original object (the copulation of the two exciting waters became a magic mirror). Narcissus is also a myth about origins: his only object was his inner primeval parents, whom he wanted to bring back to the surface of his living memory.

The French poet, Paul Valéry, wrote his "Fragments of Narcissus" composed of beautiful short poetic pieces. In "Charms" (1926), he includes passages from "Narcissus parle". He called these writings "poetry of harmony and resonance". In 1892, he wrote to André Gide *"Mon fameux Narcisse atteint des proportions...vagabondes!"*. In this poem, Narcissus is sad and nostalgic: in fact, we would say he is looking for his lost object, his original nymph, his mother Leiriope. He is trying to discover her (or perhaps his combined parents) under their original form: water. Valéry imagines Narcissus talking to the night in the light of the moon. In this nocturnal vision, his image on water is just a shadow. Was he looking for the shadow of himself? The shadow of the parental objects (the combined waters)? Or was he looking for his own shadow, which he had lost when he entered into the primal scene?

In Valéry's poem the moon plays a major role when Narcissus loses the light of the sun.

Et la lune perfide éléve son miroir
Jusque dans les secrets de la fontaine éteinte...
Jusque dans les secrets que je crains de savoir...
Jusque dans le repli de l'amour de soi-même

I am reminded of Oscar Wilde, when he tells of Narcissus looking at the fountain and asking "Why are you so sad – because I am no longer looking at myself in your beautiful mirror of crystal?". The fountain answers that it is sad because it can no longer see itself in the mirror of Narcissus's eyes. From narcissism to narcissism, from eyes to mirror, and from mirror to eyes. I recall also what Jean Cocteau once said: "A mirror should be very careful and respectful – it should *reflect* twice before *reflecting* an image...!".

As to narcissistic love, curiosity and transference, there comes to my mind a schizophrenic patient called David I had analysed for several years in London. I liked him very much, and I think he liked me too. One day he said to me "You are my shadow". This was after a long summer holiday. I had found him quite well and happy in this first session after the break. I asked him how he was feeling. He replied "You must not forget that you are my shadow". I answered "Do you mean that I was with you all the time during the holiday?". After a pause, he added "Yes, I took you home as my shadow, and developed you in the dark of the night as one does with photography. And thus I was able to have you with me projected on the wall, and moving like in a cinema film."

I then understood that David, like Valéry's Narcissus, was looking at his shadow undifferentiated from my own. In the light of the mother-moon (his sessions were in the evenings), he would become very upset as the session drew to a close and would then develop a tic – blinking his eyes. One day, with his help, I was able to understand the secret mystery of his blinking. His eyes became a photographic camera thanks to which he was able to take me in, to immobilize me, and then to bring me back to life on his own screen.

I remember his saying to me that during his first delusional break-down he felt lonely at home and very hungry. He would go to the kitchen for a glass of milk. At one point during his breakdown, as he opened the refrigerator door, his father suddenly appeared. David felt like a thief – caught in the act by the father. He then *blinked his eyes* and magically immobilized his father, changing him into a photograph. This is what he was doing to me in the transference when he felt like an empty cold refrigerator needing my presence and my warmth (maternal transfer-ence), but afraid of being caught by a persecuting superego father. The same persecuting father also became from time to time his good friend and guide, whom he wanted to take into his mental space and recreate inside his "room"/womb (the image projected on the wall, which was always under his control).

My own version of the Narcissus story would lay emphasis on the looking and becoming excited at the primal scene inside a three-dimen-sional mirror reflected on the waters. On one occasion, David became very *erotically* aroused (erotic transference) as I was talking to him (he was lying on the couch). His ears turned red, and he began to make sucking noises with his lips. I felt that he was not interested in what I was saying to him, but excited by my own noises: me, my sounds when talking, my moving in my chair, breathing... He was excited by my Echo, the shadow as it were of his own noises... Later, a similar scene took place, I said to him: "I know that it is pointless for me to give meaning to my words, when I feel the need to talk to you or to put words on your feelings." "I am not concerned today", he said, "about your noises – or even about my own. Today I just want to look." "Look at what?" I asked. He replied "Looking and getting excited when I contemplate how your thoughts copulate amongst themselves.".

Thinking of Narcissus, I can imagine my own mind as an exciting, moving fountain for David, where my little Narcissus could witness the primal scene and enter into it.

As to narcissistic wounds, I would like to illustrate my thoughts with two examples. The first is that of a woman of 47, who though she had been analysed for many years by several analysts, remained psycho-analytically chaste. I mean by this that no analysis had been able to get in touch with her narcissistic wish to preserve her chastity. We analysts tend to call such cases negative therapeutic reaction and destructive narcissism (Herbert Rosenfeld). One day, she recounted the following dream. She was in the open country, tied to a tree, it was like a circus. In front of her, there was a terrifying American Indian, perhaps a South-American Indian (!). He was shooting arrows at her, and they were coming nearer and nearer each time – she was in mortal danger. Luckily, she said, she then woke up. Her associations were that she was very much afraid of the analysis – she claimed to be feeling much better now, and wanted to interrupt the analysis with me; I was to be her last analyst. She was herself a social worker, and she used to tell me how well her patients were doing; but in her sessions, her narcissism was untouchable until the moment when my arrow-like interpretations came closer and closer to her narcissistic core. She had to leave at the very moment her narcissism was in danger of being analysed. For her, however, this meant not only wounding her narcissistic ego ideal – but in fact killing it.

In my second example, a French writer in analysis with me for several years showed strong resistances (this was her own term). She brought me a dream, which she described as "looking at a Gothic painting". In the painting, she could see a young woman, resembling herself, very tense and hard and wearing two exciting red earrings. In the background, an old woman lay – she associated this woman with her mother. In the session, she said she had heard that I had given a lecture on painting, a lecture which had interested some friends of hers very much. "I know that you are very clever," she said, "but it is very painful for me to lie down like a depressed old woman on the couch, like my mother, always sad, and listening to your remarks – I find them relevant but painful." Then she fell silent, and remained in this hard inflexible pause, like the young woman in the painting with whom she identified. Then she said: "I do not want you to talk to me, because you tell me things which I did not know before – and that I cannot stand." "What about the red earrings?" I asked. "It's like blood coming from my ears," she said. Then I added: "I am sorry to be so painful for your ears, when I touch with my words an image of yourself which cannot stand being my patient." "Oh yes, I'm split," she replied. "I want to come, but my pride will not allow me to listen; it feels so easily wounded…" I asked her for an association to Gothic art. After a pause, she said: "Gothic makes me think of *gouttes* (droplets) of blood or tears." Then I understood that her narcissistic self was allowing her to be analysed in a Gothic way – only one drop at a time.

And in this way I bring some of my own droplets of experience, my "Gothic" contribution on narcissism and narcissistic wounds in order to be in harmony with the essence of this book.

Salomon Resnik
Paris, July 1995

Preface

Working together with a co-editor is a real antidote to one's narcissism, even though the archaic wish for supremacy is constantly there waiting to assert itself. The all too familiar desire to have things done entirely one's own way and not to allow the other their contribution in their own right. If a creative outcome is to emerge one is forced to entertain the other's otherness and to tolerate their separateness.

This book grew from a paper jointly written by the editors. The article was 'The search for a primary object' and dealt with the clinical difficulties that narcissistic patients pose to their therapists and it is included in Part III of this book. The fact that when we discussed this paper at one of the Scientific Meetings of the British Association of Psychotherapists it was warmly received confirmed for us the interest that exists in the subject. It was liberating to discover how widely psychotherapists shared the experience of not being able to help these patients enough.

While working on that paper we came to realise that the recent sources of information about narcissism were mainly American including the well-known polemic between Kohut and Kernberg. So the idea of assembling a volume of collected new clinical papers by British contributors arose. During the two years since beginning work on this book we were encouraged by an apparent revival of British original thinking on the subject (Symington, *Narcissism: A New Theory*, 1993; Mollon, *The Fragile Self*, 1993; and Steiner, *Psychic Retreats*, 1993).

In selecting contributors for this book we tried to ensure that the three main British schools of psychoanalytic thought – Contemporary Freudian, Kleinian and Independent – were represented. Among them, too, we have tried to dilute the instinctive supremacy of narcissism. Salomon Resnik has said 'without difference, there is only echo'. We are grateful to all our contributors who accepted such an editing proposal.

In compiling this book our main focus has been to convey the current climate in the consulting room. Today an increasing number of patients who relied traditionally on psychiatric attention seek psychoanalytic therapeutic care. Given the demands and the needs of this sort of patient and the consequent arduous requirements on the therapist it seems important to make narcissistic patterns more clearly recognisable.

In Part I we have tried to balance a healthy scepticism for the evidence supporting psychoanalytic ideas on narcissism with a brief up-to-date presentation of the convergence of the different clinical perspectives in current therapeutic work. Clinical experience could lead to further theoretical and technical developments: the pooling of clinical experience, the hundreds of hours that each practitioner spends in his or her consulting room, if systematically collected and shared, could open the door to a more fruitful way of helping these fragile patients.

The contributions included in Part II illustrate how unresolved narcissism can affect people at different stages of their life cycle, from childhood to old age, passing through adolescence and adulthood including marriage and pregnancy.

On the whole we have avoided the polemic between narcissism being part of borderline or of psychotic phenomena. Instead, in Part III, the emphasis is on various aspects of narcissistic pathology, showing the range from the frozen sleeping states to the more openly destructive states acted out in addictions and perversions.

Narcissistic wounds are everywhere. To find oneself becomes a difficult task, when preserving good primary objects seems to be increasingly threatened. Splitting mechanisms which are the base of idealisation and denigration are strengthened by the complexity of modern life. As the contributions in this book show, to foster an adequate connection with reality including the ability to love and recognise the other, is no mean task

Judy Cooper
Nilda Maxwell
April 1995

Part I: Overviews

Chapter 1
A brief history of narcissism

DAVID LIVINGSTONE SMITH

> It is a sign of the immature state of psychology that we can scarcely utter a
> single sentence about mental phenomena which will not be disputed by
> many people.
>
> *Franz Brentano*

The landscape of narcissism is complex and rather confusing. I have
written this introduction in the hope of providing a primary orientation
and map for those wishing to explore the literature first hand. Psychoanalytic theory is not well ordered, rationally planned and signposted. It is
not, to borrow Rorty's (1986, p. 115) metaphor, like a Georgian city
'. . . of broad avenues radiating from a grand central square with the
federal government buildings, with magisterial façades and elegant capi-
tols'.

Psychoanalysis is more like:

> . . . the older medieval city of relatively autonomous neighborhoods, linked by
> small lanes that change their names half way across their paths, a city that is a
> very loose confederation of neighborhoods of quite different kinds, each with
> its distinctive internal organization, and distinctive procedures for foreign
> relations, even different conditions for entry into the federation: a city of the
> guilds, the courts of great families, religious orders and old small towns.
>
> *Rorty (1986, p. 116)*

I am not interested in providing a bare itinerary – in providing a guide-
book consisting of just names and dates. There are a number of psychoanalytic writings that do just that, although (like many writings on the
history of psychoanalytic thought) many of these turn out to be idealised
and schematic, rather like mediaeval maps that display England as the
centre of the world. I want to produce a guide that tells the reader something about why the city has grown the way it has, as well as containing
practical tips about short cuts, dead ends and rough neighbourhoods*.

*See also Bing et al. (1959); Eidleberg and Palmer (1960); Joffe and Sandler (1967); Pulver
(1970); Moore (1975); Teicholtz (1978); Kinston (1980); Macmillan (1991); Meissner (1981);
Compton (1985, 1986); Erlich and Blatt (1985); Etchegoyen (1985); Smith (1985, 1986, 1988);

Narcissism and the 'I'

Freud understood narcissism as the libidinal cathexis of the ego. To be able to understand just what Freud meant by that concise proposition we have to gain an understanding of certain aspects of his place in the history of psychology.

During Freud's formative years, the doctrine of dualism seems to have been the preferred way of conceptualising the relationship between mind and body. Over 300 years earlier Descartes had enthusiastically promoted the view that human bodies are elaborate machines operating on purely physicalistic principles, whereas human minds are ghostly, spiritual beings hovering inside time but outside space. Three forms of dualism were proposed. Some people (including Descartes) believed that the material body and the immaterial mind could influence one another. But this presented a problem. If body and mind were so radically different, how could they possibly interact? Where could the chalk of mind meet the cheese of body? Perhaps mind and body only appeared to interact. Perhaps they were merely correlated, running parallel to one another. But what miracle ensures such an exquisite correlation? Well, perhaps God, in His omniscience and omnipotence, set things up that way. By the nineteenth century, faith in religious explanations of natural phenomena had declined and a dawning neuroscience was demonstrating that events in the brain decisively influence events in the mind.

Darwin's work nudged the mind towards the natural world, and the elaboration of the principle of the conservation of energy cast doubt on the plausibility of mind–brain interaction. The last-ditch version of dualism, which was very popular in the late nineteenth and early twentieth centuries, was the view that the body (brain) influenced the mind, which was itself purely passive and could not influence the body at all.

As a young neuroscientist, Sigmund Freud was a dualist of some description. By 1895, Freud could no longer reconcile his dualism with the new clinical theories which he was developing, so he dropped dualism in favour of a more radical doctrine: physicalism. From 1895 onwards, Freud held that the mind and the brain were identical and that thought, affect and experiences are physical functions of a physical brain. There is, he thought, nothing other worldly about the mind. The mind is a part of nature and is to be studied like any other natural thing (Smith, 1992).

If the mind is just the brain, and all mental phenomena are neurophysiological phenomena, what does it mean to talk about beliefs, desires, thoughts, selves, wishes and so on? Do these things correspond to distinct brain states? Freud seems to have regarded such everyday or folk–psychological language as a regrettable necessity. Freud believed that, for a thought to become conscious, it had to forge a link with language. As our thoughts are clothed in sentences, our inner life seems to conform perfectly with the psychological expressions of our language. But this conformity is an illusion: we are prisoners of language. Our ordinary psychological language is more figurative than factual, casting a rough attributional net over experience which is good enough for ordinary life but inappropriate for scientific understanding. Freud's metapsychology was a (failed) attempt to create an alternative language for psychology.

Now let us bring this discussion back to the topic of narcissism. When Freud used the terms 'I' and 'self' he did not believe that these correspond to single and distinct entities within the mind. 'Self' talk is practically useful, but it does not tell us anything about what is really going on inside our skulls. As David Hume famously noted in the eighteenth century (and the Buddha had noted long before) that there is no item corresponding to a self anywhere inside you.

> For my part, when I enter most intimately into what I call myself, I always stumble on some particular perception or other, of heat or cold, light or shade, love or hatred, pain or pleasure. I never can catch myself at any time without a perception, and never can observe anything but the perception.
>
> *Hume (1737, p. 534)*

Although there is no self, there are self-representations. Any complex organism needs self-representations in order to keep track of itself (Dennett, 1991). In the context of his discussions of narcissism Freud characteristically used the term *'Ich'* ('I', 'ego') as a shorthand term for *'self-representation'*. So, Freud understood narcissism as a condition affecting one's self-representations.

Although Freud attempted to escape from the confines of ordinary language by placing his accounts of narcissism within the framework of metapsychology, the latter proved to be less rich and serviceable than the former. Freud described narcissism as the state of infatuation with one's own idea of oneself. From about 1909 to 1914, he believed that during earliest infancy we pass through a disorganised stage of 'autoerotism' before entering the stage of narcissism and finally the stage of object-love*. According to this story, we can manage to renounce our narcissism only by deferring it, by setting up an ideal, an 'ego ideal' promising perfection should we attain this ideal. Some, who are psychotic, find love too painful and attempt to languish in narcissism. Others, including homosexuals, love others only to the extent that they approximate their own idealised selves.

*The term 'narcissism' was used in the sexological literature of the nineteenth century. It was introduced into the psychoanalytic lexicon by Isador Sadger in 1909 (Nunberg and Federn, 1967). The first published psychoanalytic usage was in the 1910 edition of Freud's *Three Essays on the Theory of Sexuality*. Freud never publicly credited Sadger's priority.

No sooner had Freud given a detailed account of this model in 'On narcissism: an introduction' (1914) than he modified it. In 'Instincts and their vicissitudes' (1915) Freud discarded the idea of the pre-narcissistic stage and bisected the stage of narcissism. At first, the infant is preoccupied with its own pleasurable sensations: a primitive form of self-love which is unmediated by concepts of self and other. Once we are able to form an idea of our self, we automatically represent ourselves in the most flattering way imaginable. 'Self' gets equated with everything that provides enjoyment, and 'not-self' subsumes everything painful or indifferent. Learning to love means giving up this illusion of personal perfection and thereby accepting the fact of one's dependence upon others. One is narcissistic to the extent that one's self-representations encompass only those things that yield pleasure. The capacity to love is built on the capacity to find the 'bad' in oneself and the 'good' in others.

Freud changed his mind yet again in 'The ego and the id' (1923b). His remarks on this subject are so sketchy after 1923 that it is impossible to determine the extent to which he may have altered his views between 1923 and 1939. According to this story, the stage of primary narcissism is the initial representationless period. After passing through primary narcissism, the infant forms fused self/object-representations. Next, experiences of frustration force a differentiation between self- and object-representations[†]. Once these differentiations have been effected, secondary identification (identification with a prior object) becomes possible, yielding secondary narcissism.

Taken as a whole, there is a crucial ambiguity in Freud's thinking about narcissism. Sometimes, narcissism is understood positively as the infatuation with one's own self-image. At other points, however, it is understood negatively as the absence of love for others (Kinston, 1980).

In spite of frequent unannounced terminological shifts and incessant fiddling with the details, the broad outline of Freud's story of the role of narcissism in human development is quite consistent. At the start of our career as people, we have no concepts of 'me' and 'you' – we can experience states of sensual enjoyment, but cannot love ourselves or others. Once we begin to form concepts of 'me' and 'you' we fill these in tendentiously: everything good is 'me', everything that is not good is 'not-me'. In effect, we confuse self and other. It is only to the extent that we are able to draw the line between self and other realistically that we are able to love.

Klein, the Kleinians and Fairbairn

Freud thought that we move from pre-narcissism, through narcissism to a blend of narcissism and object-love. Klein was apparently the first

†In Freud's earliest model, the transition to object-love is said to be prompted by economic factors. In the second, it is apparently brought about by cognitive maturation.

analyst to claim that narcissism and object-love coexist during early infancy. Klein's proposal has *prima facie* plausibility. Small children certainly seem to love others. Like many first-string psychoanalytic theorists, Klein had a tendency towards intellectual extremism. She asserted that narcissism and object-love coexist from the very beginning of extrauterine life.

Klein believed that any plausible theory of mind must have a relational core. However, her concern with interaction was constrained by the strong internalism to which she, like Freud, adhered. Klein was less concerned with real interchanges between real people than she was with representations of such interchanges which she termed 'phantasies'. Within this framework, narcissism is just a negative moment within an object-relational dialectic. Narcissism is the upshot of identification with 'good' objects, and thus is secondary to phantasies of object-relations.

Greenson has (1969) pointed out how psychoanalysts fear new ideas. In advancing her highly original conceptions of narcissism, Klein (1952) indulged in a ritual genuflection to Freud, attempting to find anticipations of her ideas in his writings. She drew on the following passage:

> In the first instance the oral component instinct finds satisfaction by attaching itself to the sating of the desire for nourishment; and its object is the mother's breast. It then detaches itself, becomes independent and at the same time autoerotic, that is, it finds an object in the child's own body.
>
> *Freud (1923a, p. 234)*

As evidence that Freud held that object-relations precede narcissism, this is pretty weak. Freud's inconsistent use of his own terminology virtually invites such misreadings. Normally, Freud used the term *'object'* as an abbreviation for *'object-representation'* but he occasionally used it to denote a real object: a person, or a part of a person, out there in the world instead of in your head. In this passage he clearly used 'object' in the latter sense to denote a real breast of the sort that you can sink your teeth into. The mention of 'autoerotism' is neither here nor there. Although Freud did discuss the pre-narcissistic stage of autoerotism he only did so between 1911 and 1915. Before and after that period he used the term in the ordinary sense of 'masturbation', a sense that has no direct connection to the concept of narcissism. Later Kleinian writers such as Segal (1983) and Rosenfeld (1964, 1971, 1975, 1978) treated narcissism as a defence against envy*. Rather than suffer envy, the narcissist identifies with the envied object. Although insulated from the pain of envy, the narcissist pays the price of impoverished object-relations.

Fairbairn (1952) too treated human strivings and attitudes as essentially and axiomatically object-directed. Like Klein and her followers,

---

*As Segal (1983) has noted, this approach seems implicit in Klein (1957).

Fairbairn held that narcissism supervenes upon relations with internal objects. The distinction between Kleinian and Fairbairnian concepts of narcissism flows mainly from their differing views on internalisation. For Klein, internalisation is a natural and inevitable process, an intrinsic part of our mental metabolism. For Fairbairn, internalisation occurs only under the impact of frustrations experienced during the earliest phase of infantile dependence. Internal objects are therefore considered fundamentally 'bad' (tantalising or persecutory), although defensively idealised objects may be introjected to provide protection from these. For Klein, although splitting and introjection often go hand in hand, there is no necessary connection between the two. For Fairbairn, splitting (of self and object) and introjection are two features of a single process. They are structural accommodations to intense pathogenic frustrations of attachment needs during early infancy. Narcissism is always pathological, always a component of a 'schizoid' endopsychic situation.

Ferenczi and the Independents

Ferenczi was the first analyst to challenge Freud's internalism decisively. He did so by means of a new theory of omnipotence. Freud (1909) borrowed the term 'omnipotence' from the Rat Man. He used it as an abbreviation for 'the omnipotence of thought' or 'the omnipotence of wishes', both of which referred to the magical belief that one can directly influence the world by mind power alone. A few years later Freud (1912–13) linked omnipotence to narcissism[†]. To the extent that we are narcissistic, we harbour idealised self-representations. To attribute magical powers to oneself is an aspect of idealisation. The attitude of omnipotence is an offshoot of narcissism.

Just at the point that Freud had worked this out, Sandor Ferenczi (1913) proposed an alternative[*]. Ferenczi claimed that omnipotence is an interactional product. According to this story, once a baby is born, it is forced to cope with states of need. Under the influence of the pleasure principle, the infant hallucinates the breast when it is hungry but, at the same moment, its mother offers it the breast. This convergence of phantasy and reality secures for the infant a sense of its own omnipotence. The sense of one's omnipotence is the outcome of a special mother–infant choreography: it is a fully interactional phenomenon[†].

[†]Freud had not yet decided that the narcissistic stage, with its omnipotence, was a normal development. This had to wait until 'On narcissism' (Freud, 1914). Sadger acknowledged the existence of a normal narcissistic stage as early as 1909.
[*]I have suggested elsewhere (Smith, 1985) that Ferenczi's paper influenced Freud's subsequent work on narcissism.
[†]Ferenczi's developmental model presaged his interactional view of the psychoanalytic situation (Smith, 1991).

Readers familiar with the work of D.W. Winnicott will experience a feeling of *déjà vu*, because Winnicott (1951) retold Ferenczi's story, elaborating it and adding important new features (the transitional object, the magical function of play, and so on).

Michael Balint was Ferenczi's student and intellectual heir. Summing up his own position, Balint (1968) out-Kleined Klein by making the claim that Freud simultaneously sustained three distinct and mutually contradictory theories of the role of narcissism in human development. The first of these is precisely the same one that Klein attempted to foist upon Freud 16 years previously. Balint, like Klein (whose argument, by the way, he does not mention) was motivated by the desire to legitimate his own thinking through finding premonitions of it in Freud's writings. Balint had no more success than Klein in supporting his claim. Balint's 'second theory', the transition from autoerotism to narcissism to object-love, is indeed the thesis that Freud advanced between 1911 and 1915. His 'third theory', the movement from an initial stage of narcissism to a stage of object-love, is also a view which Freud espoused . . . from 1915 onwards. Balint's claim falls flat. Freud was often theoretically inconsistent, but never *that* inconsistent. Balint's own thesis elaborates a strand taken from Ferenczi's 1913 paper. Ferenczi had proposed that we only come to experience objects as distinct from ourselves when they begin to stand in our way. The first objects recognised as such by the infant are 'certain perfidious things . . . which do not obey his will' (Ferenczi, 1913, p.226). But the fact that an infant does not discriminate distinct objects does not mean that it is narcissistic. Balint called this hypothetical initial condition 'primary object-love'. It is primary object-love that precedes the individuation of objects and their subsequent introjection to produce secondary narcissism. Balint's discussion is rather confusing in that, although he speaks in the Freudian language of 'cathexis' (which is part of the discourse pertaining to mental representations), he is clearly concerned with the relationship existing between the infant and its real environment.

Federn and Kohut

Paul Federn (1977), one of the earliest members of the Vienna Psychoanalytic Society, proposed that the ego is primarily an '*erlebnis*', a lived experience. The ego is more or less co-extensive with '*Ich-Gefuhl*' ('*I-feeling*', a term found in Freud's writings and used extensively by Federn) – the sense of existing. Federn thus sharply differentiated the self-representation, which is a cognitive structure, from the felt ego. He proposed that we consider a merger with objects in terms of our felt relationship to their representations. When we merge with an object we charge its representation with '*Ich-Gefuhl*', a process that he calls

'*Verichung*' ('*egotisation*'). By the same token, the estrangement from objects is brought about by '*Entichung*' ('*de-egotisation*'). When the self-representation in de-egotised, a condition of depersonalisation ensues. Federn sometimes described primary narcissism as identical to I-feeling *per se*, and preferred to call it 'medial narcissism', after the medial or intransitive mode in Greek grammar, reserving the term 'reflexive narcissism' for the more conventional notion of narcissism as self-love. According to Federn, early in life, during the stage of the 'ego-cosmic ego', we cathect all representations with I-feeling: the whole world is felt to be continuous with us. It is only because of conflict and disappointment that the tide of ego-libido recedes, and objects are felt to exist apart from ego-feeling.

Heinz Kohut's approach to narcissism was very much in the tradition of Federn*. As with Federn, he did not regard narcissism as antithetical to object-relations. It is not the object which determines whether or not an attitude is narcissistic, it is the felt quality of the relation to that object, so 'the antithesis to narcissism is not object-relation but object-love' (Kohut, 1966, p. 429). Kohut believed that infants require experiences of unity with their (real) objects. He called these 'selfobject experiences', and came to distinguish three fundamental varieties: mirroring, idealising and twinship. 'Mirroring' refers to the presence of an admiring audience surrounding the infant. When we are mirrored, we feel the audience to be an extension of our self. 'Idealising', on the other hand, denotes the sense of immersion in another person felt to be greater than oneself. 'Twinship' involves sameness with another on one's own level†. Like Winnicott and Ferenczi, Kohut proposed that selfobject experiences require the collaboration of the infant's caretakers, rather than rising inexorably and mysteriously from within. Also, like Winnicott, Kohut believed that the infant's sense of self emerges in the context of selfobject experience and that this sense of self can only be securely established through gradual de-adaptation on the part of the parents (in Kohut's jargon, 'optimal frustration' yields 'transmuting internalisations'). The narcissistically disordered person has had insufficient or inadequate selfobject experience, and has consequently developed an enfeebled self. Such analysands are described as using the analyst as a selfobject in a narcissistic transference which reproduces infantile narcissistic states. As Kohut's work developed he found less and less use for the concept of narcissism, replacing it in the end by notions of selfobject phenomena (Kohut, 1977).

---

*According to Paul Roazen (personal communication) Federn's student, Eduardo Weiss, a man who devoted himself to the promulgation of Federn's ego psychology, was very disturbed by Kohut's failure to cite Federn.

†*How Does Analysis Cure?* (1984) Kohut had presented the twinship transference as a variety of mirror transference.

Hartmann, Jacobson, Mahler and Kernberg: psychoanalytic ego psychology

Heinz Hartmann did not propose any original theses about narcissism: he simply clarified Freud's use of the concept and offered this as a stipulative definition. In the context of his review of Freud's notion of the ego, Hartmann (1950) pointed out that, when Freud described narcissism as the libidinal cathexis of the ego, he could not have had the 1923 structural concept of the ego in mind. Hartmann plausibly claimed that taken in the context of the theory of narcissism, 'Ich' should be understood as synonymous with 'self' or, more correctly, 'self-representation'.

Edith Jacobson (1964) used Hartmann's clarification to criticise the concept of original primary narcissism. If babies exist in an undifferentiated state in which self- and object-representations have not been separated from one another, what sense does it make to talk about the libidinal cathexis of the self-representation? Although she had earlier called for the abolition of the concept of primary narcissism (Jacobson, 1954), she (1964) decided to use the term 'primary narcissism' to denote the primary undifferentiated state, a state in which 'the infant is as yet unaware of anything but his own experiences of tension and relief, of frustration and gratification' (Jacobson, 1964, p. 15), as Freud had done after 1923. With regard to the notion of secondary narcissism, Jacobson astutely criticised not so much the concept itself but Freud's use of it. Freud claimed in 'The ego and the id' (1923b) that the ego captures energy from the id by identifying with the id's sexual objects. But if such secondary identifications involve self-representation rather than the structural ego, how can this be the case?

Mahler (1967; Mahler et al., 1975) identified her stages of normal autism and normal symbiosis with Freud's stage of primary narcissism. The stage of normal autism was understood to be narcissistic in so far as it precedes the development of object-representations. The normal symbiotic stage is described as narcissistic because it coincides with undifferentiated self- and object-representations. So, Mahler's first two stages correspond roughly to the two narcissistic stages described in 'Instincts and their vicissitudes'.

Otto Kernberg (1975) defended Hartmann's stipulative definition of narcissism. Like Klein and Balint, he rejected the concept of primary narcissism. 'If . . . ,' he argued, 'the earliest investment is in a self and an object that are not yet differentiated, the concept of primary narcissism . . . is no longer warranted' (Kernberg, 1980, p. 107) and he accordingly discarded the notion of a narcissistic stage. Embroiling himself in the debate about the developmental inferences that can be legitimately derived from clinical work with narcissistically disordered adults, Kernberg (1975) claims that narcissistic character pathology is not a regression to normal infantile narcissism: it is caused by a libidinal investment in a pathological grandiose self consisting of an amalgam of real self-representations, ideal self-representations and ideal object-representations and the simultaneous repression, projection or disavowal of negatively toned self- and object-representations He also stresses that narcissistically disordered people deny difference between self and object rather than separateness as some (especially Kleinian) writers assert.

The future?

As is usually the case in psychoanalysis, there are a number of competing accounts of narcissism. How can we choose between them? With regard to the developmental stories, the results of infant research seem to support the thesis of object-relations in early infancy. Or do they? To show that infants respond to people in their immediate environment does not address the issue of whether or not the infant experiences these people as 'other'. At best, infant research falsifies the claim that infants are exclusively preoccupied with their pleasurable and unpleasurable sensations. Much of what psychoanalysts have said about narcissism seems impossible either to verify or to falsify. How can one demonstrate that a 6-month-old baby is in a state of identification with an introject of a 'good' breast? What evidence could conceivably falsify it?

Many of the theories of narcissism are not theories at all. They are not the sort of story that can be objectively evaluated against evidence*. This does not mean that they are without value. The stories about narcissism are more visions than theories†. Visions are broad accounts that define the horizons of a discipline, laying down constraints which theories are required to honour. When Klein asserted that object-relations exist from the beginning of extrauterine life, she was not proclaiming a theory (she could not validate her claim by means of evidence) – she was articulating the vision that human mental life is relational to the core.

Although visions cannot be verified or falsified, we can rationally choose between them on the basis of the success of the theories that they sanction. This is where psychoanalysis encounters a difficulty. Psychoanalysis has not made the move from visions to theories of narcissism. As we do not have testable theories of narcissism we are left with a multitude of visions. Choosing one over another becomes a very subjective matter, based on personal prejudice, aesthetic considerations or, perhaps, the preferences of one's analyst. If the psychoanalytic study of narcissism is to progress, we need to declare a moratorium on visions.

---

*There is a growing philosophical literature on the testability of psychoanalytic propositions (compare Grünbaum, 1993, for a good summary). Let those who dispute my claim that there is no way of objectively testing high-level theoretical claims about narcissism please point to such a method.

†I use the term 'vision' in much the same sense as Popper's 'metaphysical research programme'.

We need to get down to work extracting testable theories from what we have and placing these theories before the tribunal of evidence, come what may.

References

Balint M (1968). *The Basic Fault*. London: Tavistock.

Bing JF, McLaughlin F, Marburg R (1959). The metapsychology of narcissism. *Psychoanalytic Study of the Child* 14: 9–28.

Bretano F (1874). *Psychology from an Empirical Standpoint*. New York: Humanities Press, 1973.

Compton A (1985). The development of the drive object concept in Freud's work: 1905–1915. *Journal of the American Psychoanalytic Association* 33: 93–115.

Compton A (1986). Freud: objects and structure. *Journal of the American Psychoanalytic Association* 34: 561–90.

Dennett D (1991). *Consciousness Explained*. New York: Little, Brown & Co.

Eidleberg I, Palmer JN (1960). Primary and secondary narcissism. *Psychoanalytic Quarterly* 34: 480–7.

Erlich H, Blatt S (1985). Narcissism and object-love: The metapsychology of experience. *Psychoanalytic Study of the Child* 40: 57–79.

Etchegoyen R (1985). Identification and its vicissitudes. *International Journal of Psycho-Analysis* 66: 3–18.

Fairbairn WRD (1952). *Psycho-Analytic Studies of the Personality*. London: Tavistock.

Federn P (1977). *Ego Psychology and the Psychoses*. London: Karnac Books.

Ferenczi S (1913). Stages in the development of the sense of reality. In: *Selected Papers*, Vol 1. New York: Basic Books. Reprinted in 1950.

Freud S (1909). Notes upon a case of obsessional neurosis. *The Complete Psychological Works of Sigmund Freud*, standard edition, vol. 10. London: Hogarth Press.

Freud S (1912–13). Totem and taboo. *The Complete Psychological Works of Sigmund Freud*, standard edition, vol. 13. London: Hogarth Press.

Freud S (1914). On narcissism: An introduction. *The Complete Psychological Works of Sigmund Freud*, standard edition, vol. 14. London: Hogarth Press.

Freud S (1915). Instincts and their vicissitudes. *The Complete Psychological Works of Sigmund Freud*, standard edition, vol. 14. London: Hogarth Press.

Freud S (1923a). Psycho-analysis. *The Complete Psychological Works of Sigmund Freud*, standard edition, vol. 18. London: Hogarth Press.

Freud S (1923b). The ego and the id. *The Complete Psychological Works of Sigmund Freud*, standard edition, vol. 19. London: Hogarth Press.

Greenson R (1969). The origin and fate of new ideas in psychoanalysis. *International Journal of Psycho-Analysis* 50: 503–15.

Grünbaum A (1993). *Validation in the Clinical Theory of Psychoanalysis*. New York: International Universities Press.

Hartmann H (1950). Comments on the psychoanalytic theory of the ego. In: *Essays on Ego Psychology*. New York: International Universities Press. Reprinted in 1964.

Hume D (1737). *A Treatise of Human Nature*. London: Longman's. Reprinted in 1890.

Jacobson E (1954). The self and the object world. *Psycho-Analytic Study of the Child* 9: 75–127.

Jacobson E (1964). *The Self and the Object World*. London: Hogarth Press.

Joffe WG, Sandler J (1967). On some conceptual problems in the consideration of disorders of narcissism. *Journal of Child Psychotherapy* 2: 56–66.

Kernberg O (1975). *Borderline Conditions and Pathological Narcissism*. New York: Jason Aronson.

Kernberg O (1980). *Internal World and External Reality*. New York: Jason Aronson.

Kernberg O (1984). *Severe Personality Disorders*. New Haven: Yale University Press.

Kinston W (1980). A theoretical and technical approach to narcissistic disturbance. *International Journal of Psycho-Analysis* 61: 383–94.

Klein M (1952). The origins of the transference. In: *Envy and Gratitude and Other Works*. London: Hogarth Press. Reprinted in 1975.

Klein M (1957). Envy and gratitude. In: *Envy and Gratitude and Other Works*. London: Hogarth Press. Reprinted in 1975.

Kohut H (1966). Forms and transformations of narcissism. *Journal of the American Psychoanalytic Association* 14: 243–73.

Kohut H (1977). *The Restoration of the Self*. New York: International Universities Press.

Kohut H (1984). *How Does Analysis Cure?* Chicago: University of Chicago Press.

Macmillan M (1991). *Freud Evaluated: The Completed Arc*. Amsterdam: North-Holland.

Mahler M (1967). On human symbiosis and the vicissitudes of individuation. *Journal of the American Psychoanalytic Association* 15: 740–63.

Mahler M, Pine F, Bergmann A (1975). *The Psychological Birth of the Human Infant*. New York: Basic Books.

Meissner W (1981). A note on narcissism. *Psychoanalytic Quarterly* 50: 77–89.

Mollon P (1993). *The Fragile Self: The Structure of Narcissistic Disturbance*. London: Whurr Publishers.

Moore B (1975) Towards a clarification of narcissism. *Psychoanalytic Study of the Child* 30: 243–76.

Nunberg H, Federn E (Eds) (1967). *Minutes of the Vienna Psychoanalytic Society*, Vol. 2. New York: International Universities Press.

Pulver S (1970). Narcissism: the term and the concept. *Journal of the American Psychoanalytic Association* 18: 319–41.

Rorty A (1986). Self-deception, akrasia and irrationality. In: Elster J (Ed.), *The Multiple Self*. Cambridge: Cambridge University Press.

Rosenfeld H (1964). On the psychopathology of narcissism: A clinical approach. *International Journal of Psycho-Analysis* 45: 332–7.

Rosenfeld H (1971). A clinical approach to the psychoanalytic theory of the life and death instincts: an investigation into the aggressive aspects of narcissism. *International Journal of Psycho-Analysis* 52: 169–78.

Rosenfeld H (1975). Negative therapeutic reaction. In: *Tactics and Techniques in Psychoanalytic Therapy*, Vol 2: PL Giovaccini (Ed.), *Countertransference*. New York: Jason Aronson.

Rosenfeld H (1978). Notes on the psychopathology and psychoanalytic treatment of some borderline patients. *International Journal of Psycho-Analysis* 59: 215–21.

Segal H (1983). Some clinical implications of Melanie Klein's work. *International Journal of Psycho-Analysis* 64: 269–76.

Smith D (1985). Freud's developmental approach to narcissism: A concise review. *International Journal of Psycho-Analysis* 66: 489–99.

Smith D (1986). Omnipotence. *British Journal of Psychotherapy*, 3(1): 52-64.

Smith D (1988). Narcissism since Freud: towards a unified theory. *British Journal of Psychotherapy* 4: 302–12.

Smith D (1991). *Hidden Conversations: An Introduction to Communicative Psychoanalysis*. London: Routledge.

Smith D (1992) On the eve of a revolution: Freud's concepts of consciousness and the unconscious in 'Studies on hysteria' and the 'Project for a scientific psychology'. *British Journal of Psychotherapy* 9(2): 150–7.

Teicholtz J (1978) A selective review of the psychoanalytic literature on theoretical conceptualizations of narcissism. *Journal of the American Psychoanalytic Association* 26: 831–61.

Winnicott DW (1951) Transitional objects and transitional phenomena. In: *Through Paediatrics to Psycho-Analysis*. London: Hogarth Press. Reprinted in 1958.

Chapter 2
The current state of clinical work: diagnosis, treatment and outcome

JUDY COOPER AND NILDA MAXWELL

Diagnosis

Why do we need diagnostic criteria for narcissism given that exact diagnosis is not necessary to begin treatment? The problem with narcissistic patients is their unassailability and their increasing demands on therapeutic resources. It would seem that narcissistic patients are equated with a very damaged object which is either the depleted/devouring breast or the damaged combined parental imago. What the narcissistic patient is unable to get from his primary object, he transfers with insatiable intensity to his analyst.

These features may often be apparent from previous therapeutic failures but otherwise they only become evident as the treatment progresses. Owing to the fact that the libidinal energy of narcissistic patients is chiefly spent in trying to repair damaged objects in their inner world, they appear entirely absorbed by this task and there is not much room for external reality or including the other's presence.

Can analysis really make a difference to this type of patient? The ones Freud did not want to touch and had traditionally landed up in psychiatric hospitals?

As more recent British publications have suggested, what is needed for working with these patients is either specialised further training (as in the USA) or highly experienced analysts/therapists with more than 10 years expertise (as in the UK).

Even experienced analysts acknowledge difficulties in assessing the depth of narcissistic disturbance until patients are well into treatment. It would seem that this is not altogether surprising because narcissistic patients so often put so much investment into their façade. Symptoms cover up deep pathology and frequently there is little to indicate any serious or deep-seated disturbance (Sandler et al., 1991; Glasser, 1992), what in Winnicott's terms has been referred to as the false self covering the true self (Winnicott, 1960). As one experienced analyst acknowledged: 'I only realise I am dealing with one of these patients when he is lying on the couch after leaving a knife on the chair.'

> Narcissistic wounds are special kinds of hurts – those that cut to the quick, that assail us where we live, that threaten our identity or our self-image, or our ego-ideal or our self-esteem. They are the hurts that go to the core. The emotional response to narcissistic injury is hurt, shame, and rage.
>
> *Levin (1993, p. xiv)*

Narcissistic difficulties involve disturbance in the experience of the self. It is important to discriminate between different degrees of severity. There is a vast difference between someone labelled mildly narcissistic and someone who is severely narcissistically disturbed and this will obviously reflect in the outcome of the treatment. Although the surface manifestations may vary and a person may display hysterical, obsessional or phobic symptoms, or even present what looks like a manic phase of a cyclic illness, the narcissist's core is split and feels dead. Other authors refer to this core emphasising grandiosity (Kohut) or aggression (Kernberg) (Russell, 1985). We believe that narcissistic disturbances could be grouped in three main categories:

1. The empowered or 'phallic' narcissist
2. The manipulative narcissist (sometimes thought of as 'psychopathic')
3. The impoverished narcissist (sometimes referred to as 'borderline').

Among all the variables that are associated with the narcissistic personality, we have chosen their immense difficulty in acknowledging dependency and have based these different types on this criterion. All three types present tremendous difficulty in accepting dependency but each type varies as to how they deal with this.

The empowered narcissist (phallic)

Although successful, their achievements have the function of supporting their self-image and conferring a sense of power. They tend to be hard and ruthless and their grandiosity is upheld by their being able to maintain an admiring response from others to their superiority. They are frequently charismatic, leading and organising others. Their impressive schemes often dazzle with their success but ultimately are not sustainable. Fostering personal relationships is irrelevant to their master plan.

The manipulative narcissist (psychopathic)

With their charming and often seductive façade, they have the ability to detect others' needs and to feed off these. They appropriate the usefulness of the other. Living in an atmosphere of excited expectation that things are always about to happen, they appear to be optimistic. Their phantasies of success serve to provide the scaffolding for their grandiosity.

The disempowered narcissist (borderline)

Even when they *do* achieve, they cannot feel supported by their accomplishments. They appear not to be able to incorporate anything good because they have nowhere to put it (Resnik, 1995). They have feelings of low self-esteem accompanied in severe cases by fragmentation and identity confusion. However, the grandiose hallmark of the narcissistic personality is patently there behind a different façade.

A person can fluctuate either way between their adjacent categories (see Table below), so the manipulative can waver to impoverishment and visa versa, whereas the phallic includes the manipulative dimension always and the manipulative group could have fleeting phallic achievements. The distinction is one of degree. The empowered narcissist is not all powerful and the disempowered is not completely powerless. Essentially, in the case of the phallic types, their narcissistic injury is to some extent compensated for by their achievements and lifestyle, whereas the the borderline narcissist, in spite of efforts to achieve a position of power, remains with deep feelings of powerlessness.

	Empowered	Manipulative	Disempowered
Sense of self	Precarious with obvious grandiosity	Precarious with wavering evidence of grandiosity	Precarious with no awareness of pervading unconscious grandiosity
Relatedness to others			
Quality:	Contemptuous	Multiple/superficial	When it happens: dependency and symbiosis
Style:	Control and power	Seductive/ manipulative	Fearful/passive
Goal achievement	High	Mainly fantasising	If it happens it is of no account to them

As Symington (1993) rightly points out: 'None of us is free from narcissism, and one of the fundamental aspects of the condition is that it blinds us to self-knowledge' (p. 10). Clinical experience currently agrees on listing five diagnostic criteria for narcissistic disturbances:

1. A grandiose sense of self-importance or uniqueness

2. A preoccupation with phantasies of unlimited success, power, brilliance, beauty or ideal love
3. Exhibitionism, the person requires constant attention and admiration
4. Cool indifference or naked feelings of rage: 'narcissistic rage', inferiority, shame, humiliation or emptiness in response to criticism or defeat
5. At least two of the following characteristics of disturbances in interpersonal relationships: entitlement (expectation of special favours without assuming reciprocal responsibilities), interpersonal exploitativeness, relationships that characteristically alternate between the extremes of over-idealisation and devaluation, lack of empathy and need to control.

Although it is acknowledged that narcissistic personalities may function extremely well socially, this is at a very surface level and beneath this veneer lies a ruthless disregard for others (Kernberg, 1975, p. 225). They are rarely guilty but always ashamed, constantly trying to live up to stringent ego-ideal prescriptions which should not be confused with super-ego demands.

Body

As in the Narcissus myth, these patients are either deeply in love with their own image as it stands, or believe that they can attain their ideal physical image one way or another (dieting, exercising, muscle building, plastic surgery, colon irrigation and so on). Their image can always be better and pain is forgotten in this frantic search to attain their phantasy of physical perfection. Gender transformation is an extreme manifestation of this search for physical perfection. Implantation or removal of body parts is increasingly endorsed by our culture as legitimate ways of pursuing this goal. All these manoeuvres seem to express a concrete search for a better breast (e.g. silicone implants, cosmetic mastectomies) or a displaced one (e.g. face lifts, body lifts, nose corrections, penis alterations).

Habitat/space

In our experience, this type of patient often lives in a transitional space. This is not in the Winnicottian sense of facilitating development, but, rather, in a way that stultifies any development. As Steiner (1993) said they find 'home' in external structures. Home is a shelter, a fortress, a carapace skin, so it is often a retreat where no one is allowed in and a state of limbo is ensured. Those who are never comfortable inside these structures become claustrophobic, and those who are never comfortable outside them become agoraphobic. None of them can accept limits: this would mean the end of the illusion which is what sustains them. Any move towards establishing a permanent residence is experienced as threatening. They feel any change as catastrophic because they have had no holding to enable them to organise any real change. Indeed, some patients will retaliate if they feel under pressure to get settled. This was shown by a divorced patient who moved into the student quarters of the hospital where he worked and finally moved into his own home after a few years of therapeutic work, only to have an intense negative therapeutic reaction during which he wanted to end his treatment.

Time

Difficulties with time are never more evident than in the conviction with which these patients present their narcissistically invested projects. There is an elational and grandiose aura about these projects which have no reference to the passing of time or concept of age or death. A current illustration is the prevalent phantasy of a limitless age for fertility which is being encouraged by the scientific findings in this area. There are well-known cases of men and women believing that they will still have large families when they have not even started at 50 years of age. Alongside their unshakeable convictions of this kind, there is an indecisiveness and inertness and everything is conflictual, so that very often nothing moves.

Basic to this narcissistic way of thinking is the belief that it is the infant who creates and controls the good object. This illusion allows them to deny the primal facts of life which in Money-Kyrle's (1968) terms are the following:

1. The chief source of goodness required for an infant's survival resides outside him in the external world. This refers to acknowledging the separateness between self and object.
2. The recognition of the parents' intercourse as a supremely creative act. This refers to an acceptance of the Oedipal situation.
3. The recognition of the inevitability of time and ultimately of death. This means that all good things have to come to an end, and that access to the breast cannot go on for ever.

Money-Kyrle believes that coming to terms with these primal facts of life, without misrepresenting or distorting them, offers a measure of mental health. We know that narcissistic resistance will put up strong armour against acknowledging or working through these basic facts of life.

Treatment

In August 1967 Anna Freud writing to Kohut (Cocks, 1994, p. 171) refers to the widening of the field of psychoanalytic treatment. She states that the transference neuroses are easier to treat than the other mental disturbances called 'narcissistic disorders'. She alerts one to the 'impasses into which treatment runs if the narcissistic phenomena are treated on a par with the transference neurosis symptomatology'.

Unlike the borderline and psychotic patients both of whom experience empathy as threatening, the narcissistic patient is continually searching for merger to substantiate his fragile core. With these patients the analyst will get nowhere if he continues to work as if he is being cathected as an object. Confrontation, pointing out reality, problem-solving are not effective. In Kohut's terms, change is only possible if the patient can bear to experience the analyst as a 'selfobject'.

As with the treatment of children, Anna Freud felt that the analyst is rather used and 'drawn into' the patient's 'milieu':

> The patient uses the analyst not for the revival of object-directed strivings, but for inclusion in a libidinal (i.e. narcissistic) state to which he has regressed or at which he has become arrested.
>
> *Cocks (1994, p. 171)*

It has been observed that very often the therapist is considered as a vehicle to be transformed magically and immediately by the patient's phantasies into a good or bad, protective or persecutory aspect of their internal world.

Turning to the Kleinian viewpoint, Hanna Segal (1983) in her paper 'Emergence from narcissism' tried to delineate Melanie Klein's contribution to this subject. As she states Klein made only two direct statements about narcissism and Segal found that implicit in Klein's reference was an 'intimate relation between narcissism and envy. . . To me envy and narcissism are like two sides of a coin. Narcissism defends us against envy . . .' (Segal, 1983, p. 270). Envy is so wounding given that it involves acknowledging that we are lacking what the other has. Envy implies that there is enough differentiation between self and object so as to allow a sense of deprivation. Rosenfeld, as part of this tradition, made a specifically British contribution (Mollon, 1993) to the study of narcissism where the concept of envy seems transformed from its initial formulation. Instead, he put forward the first description of a destructive mental organisation, an 'internal mafia', which he said accounts for the intense persecutory feelings of these patients. Similar formulations along the lines of narcissism as part of a defensive organisation are found in O'Shaughnessy (1981), Sohn (1985) and Steiner (1987). Although the usefulness of interpreting envy has become increasingly doubtful (Rosenfeld, 1987), the new concepts prove to be far more effective in the treatment of these patients.

The perfect fit

The subjective aspects of the patient–therapist 'fit' are particularly important for this group of patients (Higgitt and Fonagy, 1992; Rayner, 1992).The need for attunement of these patients manifests itself in different ways, e.g. their intense demand to understand and be under-stood. Also, it is very important to keep the contract, the setting and the frame as steady and consistent as possible: to establish a 'rhythm of safety' (Grotstein et al., 1987). This safety refers to the tempo of the interpretations too: the therapist should be alert to vague or badly timed interpretations, as well as to whether they are too specific in an affec-tively charged way. Steiner (1993) quotes a patient who was 'stimulated to a violent attack when it seems I went too far or too fast' with the inter-pretations (p. 74). Quick analytic responses could be taken as a refusal to accept their projections and the feeling that their material is thrown back to them is taken as rejection. To create a therapeutic milieu where the patient feels safe, some analysts not only insist on delaying interpre-tations until a patient is ready for them, but minimise any expectation that they will have a mobilising function. It is generally believed that treatment should focus on the present whether this involves clarifica-tions or looking at the therapeutic relationship. Mancia (1993) points out other difficulties in accepting interpretations. He shows how these patients act out inside the analytic setting by taking what they receive as their own:

> O's robberies occur in practically every session: the stolen object is the power and wisdom that he thinks is conferred by analysis on whoever possesses the method: put in simpler terms, my interpretations. O appears to accept my interpretation collaboratively, but instead of reflecting about it, metabolizing it, and using it for mental growth, he transforms it, manipulates it, and hands it back to me to demonstrate that my interpretation is incomplete, that he is much better at interpreting than I am, and that he does not need my work: he can do it alone . . . it makes no difference whether analysis is carried out with or without me, because he obviously wishes to negate every valuable aspect of the analytic experience . . . together with any painful feeling related to acknowledging my presence, his need for me, and the fear of separation.
>
> *Mancia (1993, pp. 60, 64)*

These patients act out inside the analytic setting by 'stealing' what one gives them. They cannot acknowledge what they receive, rather claiming it as their own property. Sohn (1985) in turn has suggested that as a patient progresses in analysis 'he begins to feel that he has been robbed of his previously held special powers and that the robbery has been perpetrated by the analyst during the analysis' (p. 204). They cannot accept anything that they have not generated and which comes from outside themselves. They are bent on their own modes of self-cure (Khan, 1974, 1979).

Given the extreme difficulty that these patients experience with the passage from the merged to the separated state, some analysts feel that it is essential to try and keep a modicum of availability and continuity going even in the holiday breaks. This is to counteract the tendency in these patients to act out their uncontained, overwhelming feelings at the terrifying experience of being on their own. Counter to this, other analysts maintain an extremely tight frame, similar to the environment that these patients have created in their own defensive organisation, so that the patient may feel protected from his or her own dread of chaos and more able to distinguish phantasy from reality. However, when this relationship is carried out in a flexible way, contacting the patient if necessary, e.g. following absences or holiday breaks, hospital visits, appropriate self-disclosure, etc. are not precluded as part of the treatment.

Dealing with aggression

The main differences in the treatment approaches of the three schools that we distinguish (Freudian, Kleinian and Independent) appear to be in their dealings with aggression. This controversy can be seen to go back to the Freud–Klein debate. Primitive impulses, persecution and mockery become genuine and real for these patients. The analyst should be able to withstand a patient's enraged and hostile transference as well as to tolerate the distortions about themselves and their reality coming from the patient's deeply split ego. As Freud said:

> the ego can be split . . . as a crystal thrown to the floor, it breaks but not into haphazard pieces. It comes apart along lines of cleavage into fragments whose boundaries, though they were invisible, were predetermined by the crystal structure.
>
> *Freud (1932, pp. 58–9)*

In describing the structure of the narcissist's inner world, dominated by splitting and projective identification, some authors also include self-destructiveness, profound depression, grandiosity, dependency, envy and contempt. This last dimension has been explored at length by Grunberger (1989) who emphasises the anal component in narcissistic contempt.

Narcissistic transference and narcissistic rage

Today, much is written about transference psychosis. This refers to psychosis *in* the transference where the patient loses his sense of self, and his confusion is accompanied by unremitting hostility expressed by passivity or attacks on the analyst (Nissim Momigliano and Robutti, 1992). The narcissistic transference is somewhat different. With these patients highlighting regression, dependency or defences could lead to 'symbiotic relatedness'. Seinfeld (1993), referring to the handling of negative therapeutic reaction, quotes the writings of Giovacchini and Searles in the 1950s – they both emphasised the therapeutic value of the symbiotic transference. This is in line with Balint's (1968) concept of 'benign regression' and Winnicott's of the regressive symbiotic transference as a psychic rebirth (1963). Seinfeld details the stages of symbiotic transference: idealised, ambivalent and finally resolution.

The three main schools that we have distinguished all try to disentangle the confused aspects of the self and to reduce the patient's high levels of anxiety. Each has a different approach in dealing with this crucial aspect of the treatment: the Kleinian school, mainly through Rosenfeld and other neo-Kleinians, believe that the primitive splitting and aggression of the transference psychosis can only be worked through by constantly interpreting and exposing the violent and sado-masochistic aspects of the transference relationship so that they can be integrated into the ego. Kernberg, on the other hand, coming from a classical position, although he has taken much from the Kleinians, insists on limiting the excesses of aggressive behaviour during analysis. He feels that the analyst should actively block this behaviour, establishing rules and limits whenever the safety of the treatment is endangered. Kohut, for his part, whose main ideas are very much on a par with the British Independent School, considers what the other schools define as pathological narcissism as various stages of immature narcissism or selfobject relating (merger, mirroring, idealised). What the others consider transference psychosis becomes, for Kohut, developmental pathways not experienced in childhood which can be reopened and connected through adequate mirroring. The vicissitudes of the self–selfobject unit are the vicissitudes of the child–parent dyad fitting together or failing to do so. In the treatment this re-enactment often results in a negative therapeutic reaction. Kohut says that the question to be asked is:

> . . . whether or not the patient is able to develop a selfobject transference when the opportunity to re-experience the selfobject of childhood is offered to him in the psychoanalytic situation. If the answer is yes, we will diagnose the patient as a 'narcissistic personality disorder', if the answer is no, we will diagnose him as 'borderline' . . . The line is not an immovable one.
>
> *Kohut (1984, p. 219, note 7)*

As Kohut sees it, a person can be brought from immature selfobject relating to more mature ways of selfobject relating and, in the best cases, to separateness.

Much has been said about the limited range of affects of the narcissistic patient. They seem to yo-yo between anger and fear. The areas of feeling they *do* have and experience quite deeply are (1) the pain relating to their narcissistic injuries (schizoids never stop complaining) and (2) a sadistic awareness of what will hurt the other. Symington (1993) quotes Bergson: 'How does the wasp know how to sting in the right place?' It would appear that they 'feel' with minute precision where to sting in order to paralyse their objects without totally incapacitating them.

Kohut (1972) has emphasised narcissistic rage. He understood this *not* as pathological but as the justified response to injuries from which children cannot recover by themselves. Masud Khan's famous contribution (1974) on the concept of 'cumulative trauma' refers to the repeated experience of narcissistic injury. Khan was talking about the accumulation of relatively minor injuries whereas Kohut was dealing with the accumulation of more severe ones (Levin, 1993).

The different traits of the narcissist's personality that challenge the continuity and progress of the analytic treatment are represented in the myth of Narcissus who confused image and reality. What Narcissus saw mirrored in the water was the perfect lover he was longing for. The difficulties in grasping reality and the avoidance of self-knowledge, what have been referred to as the main active process of splitting in the narcissistic patient, have expression in the consulting room. First, it shows in a remarkable lack of connectedness with the analyst and, second, in a longing for a perfect fit. So, self-knowledge is avoided because it involves the destruction of the perfect image (Hamilton, 1982). This turning away from reality prepares the way for 'unreality' to take over.

Outcome

In our view the positive outcome of treatment could range from (1) using the narcissistic selfobject relationship in a positive way (Kohut) to (2) aiming for object-relationships with a decreasing degree of contempt that requires a shift in the inner structure (or object-relations) which is not always achievable (Kernberg, Fairbairn). This second more pessimistic view admits that even after treatment these patients still retain a degree of contempt for the object. The aim of increasing their social adaptability is, therefore, more realistic. However, (3) the Kleinian position emphasises working through the paranoid–schizoid splits until the mixed feelings of the depressive position are bearable and the reparative potential can emerge. Through this process the narcissist's powerful internal defensive organisation will be eroded and eventually given up.

Kohut writing to Khan in 1969 (23 September) (Cocks, 1994, p. 241) acknowledged the Kleinians as 'those who have committed themselves to the empathic immersion into the earliest states of mind'. This is undoubtedly true and, therefore, their contribution with this group of patients has been considerable in understanding them. Therapists belonging to other theoretical schools have taken from the Kleinian schema and benefited from it.

When dealing with severely narcissistic patients one must decide on one's aim in treatment: either to erode the enormous destructive ability of these patients or to work on fostering the more creative aspects of narcissism. On the whole, the Kleinians choose the first option whereas the contemporary Freudians and the Independents tend to work with the second.

The degree of insight of these patients is variable and the therapist should be prepared to face complete lack of insight but this need not stand in the way of some change. As Rey (1994) underlined there is a schizoid way of being. If this is felt to be accepted, there may be different positive outcomes. Sometimes containment in the analysis gets rid of the more incapacitating aspects of grandiosity even if some elements of it remain. This would seem to be the case when the therapist tries to encourage and stretch every inch of his or her patient's developmental possibility. One must bear in mind that the developmental process is against these patients; as they age, the danger of this pathology increases given that the defences cease to be effective and the reservoir of libidinal energy gradually dries up. Mid-life is a point of vulnerability, and statistical material shows that attempted suicide is more frequent in this group of female patients who are in their thirties. Therapists are well acquainted with the narcissist's attempt to ally with the instincts (searching for the object), but because of the difficulties with connectedness, they frequently latch on to the ritual dance of life and death.

So much therapeutic energy with these patients goes into 'damage limitation'. There are phases when to avoid further deterioration becomes the primary aim of treatment. At these times anchoring them more securely in the real world (Bion, 1967) becomes a priority. The therapeutic investment then becomes absorbed in attempting to unveil, inch by inch, a little more reality, making it possible for the patient to use it.

With the progress of treatment it is possible to see some inner shift which allows more psychic flexibility and a little more room for the other. The slowness of the rate of change and the narrow margins of it should alert therapists to decide on their own suitability to treat this kind of patient. As Padel (1977, p. 1439) said:

> The psychoanalytic set-up is a bi-polar system in which both the members bear joint responsibility for change, good or bad, for lack of change, and – within limits – for the rate of change.

He adds that the way to develop a deeper understanding of these patients is by 'analysing the partial failures and not labelling them partial successes'.

Obviously, the expectations and outcome of treatment for the narcissistic patients vary according to the severity of the disturbance. Through analysis these patients can preserve or improve their surface adaptation and social functioning. Kohut, who pioneered this kind of rehabilitation, insisted on minimising the 'cosmetic solution' (false self). He preferred to foster creatively a use of the narcissistic grandiosity in the service of the more genuine aspects of the self, and thereby develop the ability to accept pleasure. Somehow, with severely narcissistic disturbance, one may have to accept that the therapeutic result will never achieve a pure object-relations solution but lie somewhere in between object-relations and purely narcissistic relating. Kohut (1984) calls this 'mature selfobject relations'.

Symington, in his *New Theory of Narcissism* concludes that truly narcissistic individuals, however gifted, are able to cause considerable damage to the social structures to which they belong – to their families, their work organisations, clubs, societies (Symington, 1993, p. 10). For this reason, Symington feels that highly narcissistic people should never be appointed to key posts or senior positions. However, they frequently are. Symington's conclusion on the destructive effects of narcissism in all social structures is relevant in the specific case of the family. When these patients do have children, clinical evidence shows that they cannot foster the process of separate development. They disempower their children, experiencing them merely as an extension of themselves. Follow-up research shows that there are differences in outcome for males and females. Males seem to have more difficulty in marrying than females. And females, intent on preserving the symbiotic bond with their partners, do manage to sustain a relationship but frequently have difficulties in having children. As it has been said: 'The world is pretty much run by narcissistic personality disorders . . . they can usually "perform"' (Levin, 1993, p. 242).

References

Balint M (1968). *The Basic Fault: Therapeutic Aspects of Regression*. London: Tavistock.

Bion WR (1967). *Second Thoughts*. London: Heinemann. Reprinted in 1984 by Karnac Books, London.

Cocks G (Ed.) (1994). *The Curve of Life: Correspondence of Heinz Kohut*. Chicago: University of Chicago Press.

Freud S (1932). The dissection of the psychical personality. *The Complete Psychological Works of Sigmund Freud*, standard edition, vol. 22. London: Hogarth Press, 1962.

Glasser M (1992). Problems in the psychoanalysis of certain narcissistic disorders. *International Journal of Psycho-Analysis* 73: 493–503.

Grotstein JS, Lang JA, Solomon MF (Eds) (1987). *The Borderline Patient: Emerging Concepts in Diagnosis, Psychodynamics and Treatment*. Hillsdale, NJ: The Analytic Press.

Grunberger B (1989). *New Essays on Narcissism*. London: Free Association Books.

Hamilton V (1982). *Narcissus and Oedipus*. London: Routledge & Kegan Paul. Reprinted in 1984 by Karnac Books, London.

Higgitt A, Fonagy P (1992). Psychotherapy in borderline and narcissistic personality disorder. *British Journal of Psychiatry* 161: 23–43.

Kernberg O (1975). *Borderline Conditions and Pathological Narcissism*. New York: Jason Aronson.

Khan MMR (1974). *The Privacy of the Self*. London: Hogarth Press.

Khan MMR (1979). *Alienation in Perversions*. London: Hogarth Press. Reprinted in 1993 by Karnac Books, London.

Kohut H (1972). Thoughts on narcissism and narcissistic rage. *Psychoanalytic Study of the Child* 27: 360–400.

Kohut H (1984). *How Does Analysis Cure?* Chicago: University of Chicago Press.

Levin JDL (1993). *Slings and Arrows: Narcissistic Injury and Its Treatment*. New York: Jason Aronson.

Mancia M (1993). *In the Gaze of Narcissus*. London: Karnac Books.

Mollon P (1993). *The Fragile Self: The Structure of Narcissistic Disturbance*. London: Whurr Publishers Ltd.

Money-Kyrle R (1968). Cognitive development. *International Journal of Psycho-Analysis* 49: 691–8.

Nissim Momigliano L, Robutti A (1992). *Shared Experience: The Psychoanalytic Dialogue*. London: Karnac Books.

O'Shaughnessy E (1981). A clinical study of a defensive organisation. *International Journal of Psycho-Analysis* 62: 359–69.

Padel J (1977). The creative narcissist. *Times Literary Supplement*: December 9th, p. 1439.

Rayner E (1992). Matching, attunement and the psychoanalytic dialogue. *International Journal of Psycho-Analysis* 73: 39–54.

Resnik S (1995). *Mental Space*. London: Karnac Books.

Rey H (1994). In: J Magagna (Ed.), *Universals of Psychoanalysis and the Treatment of Borderline and Psychotic States*. London: Free Association Books.

Rosenfeld H (1987). *Impasse and Interpretation*. London: Routledge.

Russell GA (1985). Narcissism and the narcissistic personality disorder: A comparison of the theories of Kernberg and Kohut. *British Journal of Medical Psychology* 58: 137-48.

Sandler J, Person E, Fonagy P (Eds) (1991). *On Narcissism: An Introduction*. New Haven, London: Yale University Press.

Segal H (1983). Some clinical implications of Melanie Klein's work. Emergence from Narcissism. *International Journal of Psycho-Analysis* 64: 269–76.

Seinfield J (1993). *The Bad Object Handling Negative Therapeutic Reaction in Psychotherapy*. New York: Jason Aronson.

Sohn L (1985). Narcissistic organization, projective identification and the formation of the identificate. *International Journal of Psycho-Analysis* 66: 201–13.

Steiner J (1987). The interplay between pathological organisations and the paranoid-schizoid and depressive positions. *International Journal of Psycho-Analysis* 68: 69–80.

Steiner J (1993). *Psychic Retreats*. London: Routledge.

Symington N (1993). *Narcissism: A New Theory*. London: Karnac Books.

Winnicott DWW (1960). Ego distortion in terms of true and false self. In: *The Maturational Processes and the Facilitating Environment*. London: Hogarth Press, 1965. Reprinted in 1990 by Karnac Books, London.

Winnicott DWW (1963). Dependency in infant-care, in child-care, and in the psycho-analytic setting. In: *The Maturational Processes and the Facilitating Environment*.London: Hogarth Press, 1965. Reprinted in 1990 by Karnac Books, London.

Part II: Narcissism in the Life Cycle

Chapter 3
Early problems in mother–child separation as a basis for narcissistic disturbance

MARIA POZZI

Introduction

In this chapter I am going to look at one of the possible origins of narcissism as it begins to emerge in the early relationship between mother and child. This topic will be approached from the Kleinian point of view which has helped me to throw some light on the mother's and the child's psychology in interaction. I will describe two short psychotherapeutic interventions with young children aged under 5 years and their families. In both situations the focus will be on the partial failure to meet the child's emotional developmental needs and special attention will be given to the problem of differentiation and separation. The separation difficulty seems to be intensified by the lack or inadequacy of either the father's presence or a paternal function within the mother.

The dead baby

'He has always avoided looking at my eyes since being a baby at the breast,' said Mrs Smith, the mother of two-and-a-half-year-old Peter. When I asked what she thought he might have seen in her eyes, she replied: 'Sadness as I always thought of Duncan.' Her first child, born in her previous marriage, had died of a congenital disease before he was 2 years old.

In the family sessions mother reported that, after Duncan's death, she had had a psychic experience in which she was leaving her body behind and 'was going to die', in order to be with her first baby whom she had loved so much. Intense separation anxieties and difficulties in mourning Duncan had greatly affected Mrs Smith's relationship with Peter. She became aware that she had never looked at Peter as Peter but as if he were Duncan. Peter was referred to the Under 5's Counselling Service of a provincial Child Guidance Clinic because of nightmares, demanding-

31

ness and tantrums when he had to separate from mother to go to nursery. All this had started a couple of months before the birth of baby Lucy, who was 7 months old at the time of the family's first visit to the clinic.

Peter showed clear signs of jealousy both with Lucy at home and with the children at the nursery. He was isolated, unable to play with them and, when mother collected him after a few hours, he would run away from her, hide and refuse to go home. He was described as always avoiding mother's eyes and of preferring his blanket for solace rather than allowing mother to comfort him. He had a slightly better relationship with his father. In the sessions Peter behaved as if he were in the nursery as he flopped by himself in a corner, then turned away avoiding mother's gaze and mine. I noticed the striking similarity between his dead-looking eyes and mother's depressed eyes. I was also told that he wanted to be called by his sister's name and to dress as a girl. The mother's response to Peter was of deep disappointment, hurt, jealousy and rage as he was not a 'normal child' or a 'perfect child' as she was able to tell me.

Mrs Smith had not been able to mourn the loss of her first baby or possibly the failure of her first marriage. She had turned to Peter both as a replacement of Duncan and as the vessel for her feelings, expectations, projections and denial of Duncan's death. Peter had turned away from her since the early days and had used a blanket as a total substitute of mother: he held on to it, dragged it along with him all the time in the absence of an object that received, contained, transformed and returned the projections of the child to the child himself (Bion, 1963). Mother's depression and baby Peter's depression went along hand in hand, unnoticed and in what seemed to me to be a symbiotic way, until separation at the nursery became a 'must'. At that point Peter had not developed a sense of his own self or the inner goodness and strength that allow children to grow, to face separation from mother, to deal with the arrival of new babies, etc. He began to demand of mother a great deal and yet rejected her and was angry with her as if he was aware of never having had a properly functioning maternal figure. A vicious circle had been set up when mother, who also was filled with anger and resentment towards Peter, consulted the Clinic for help.

Here we see how mother's need to be helped over a bereavement, to be looked after and taken care of have been acted out unconsciously in her relationship with her little child. He had become stuck at the point of being a separate individual and of becoming more independent from mother.

In the eight sessions Mr and Mrs Smith had – some sessions were with both children, some with Peter and not the baby, some with the parents alone – Mrs Smith was able to explore, to air and to think of those painful issues, which she had always kept away from her husband so as to protect their marriage. She could understand and withdraw her projections from Peter and begin to mourn the loss of her first baby. She was then able 'to see' Peter as Peter, for the first time ever. She had previously mirrored herself in her child's eyes and mind rather than the other way round, i.e. to be there for the baby to see himself in mother's eyes. Lovely sparkles, smiles and a link with the world began to appear in both mother's and son's eyes and their dead and switched-off look went. The mutual rejection decreased, physical closeness began as mother reported and as it was seen in the sessions. Father visited the new lands of his wife's and child's experience and proved to be very supportive, thoughtful and grateful.

Maternal ambivalence in separating from her toddler

In this section I shall describe in detail the history and evolution of a separation problem that involved Mrs Green and her three-and-a-half-year-old daughter (Pozzi, 1993). Poppy – already at the age of 8 months – would become particularly distressed when strangers looked at her. At 3 years and 4 months she used to be so distraught when left by her mother at the nursery, that she decided to give up taking Poppy there. Instead they came to the Child and Family Clinic of the provincial town where I was working as a child psychotherapist at that time. Mother and child had struck me from our first encounter in the waiting-room, because of the atmosphere of 'old times' that they created around them. A chubby 3 year old with dark curls, blue eyes, dressed in Laura Ashley lace and flowery clothes, and an elegant but somewhat diaphanous and pale lady seemed to have popped out of an illustrated fairy-tale book.

The main problem – as it soon emerged – was that Poppy could not be left by her mother at the nursery or at a neighbour's house because she was terrified of children of both her own age and other ages. As a baby Poppy wanted to be fed all the time and the feeding had felt like a never-ending experience, reported Mrs Green. Poppy was breast-fed but also always had bottles of orange juice or water as she had been a very thirsty baby. When mother, feeling exhausted, stopped breast-feeding, Poppy took to the beaker easily. Not much more was recounted about her early days. However, mother told me, in a rather casual way, that she had recently had a miscarriage and had given up trying to conceive again, as a result of her preoccupation with Poppy and being too busy with her. Mrs Green believed that the nursery teachers could not handle Poppy's difficulties because they were too busy with other children. She was also under the tyrannical control of Poppy, who could only be left with an elderly lady who lived 100 miles away, every time mother had to do something for herself, e.g. go to the dentist.

When Mrs Green finally spoke about the miscarriage, after I broached the issue, she became visibly upset in the session and began to cry. The baby should have been born a few weeks later. Poppy soon bit her tongue while eating crisps and she, too, began to cry and was consoled by mother who sat her on her lap. It seemed to me that Poppy, too, had to find a reason to cry to be identified with mother. This seemed to be aimed at avoiding separateness rather than at getting attention. Also in spite of Mrs Green's insistence that Poppy had not known about the pregnancy, Poppy produced a startling play in which she acted as a pregnant woman, lying open-legged on the floor, pressing her hands on her naked tummy and moving it up and down as if wanting to push something out. When I verbalised this play, Poppy shied away and mother said that she had played in a similar way for the past few weeks. Again Poppy seemed to be acting, in a non-separate way, like a mother who should soon have given birth to a baby.

What was miscarried was a baby and also the session on the week when the baby should have been born. However, as no birth had taken place, Mrs Green decided not to insist on Poppy going to nursery: her distress at the moment of separation was unbearable to Mrs Green. My idea that the miscarriage had produced not a new baby but a 'baby' Poppy was accepted and confirmed by Mrs Green. Poppy had wanted to wear nappies for the past 3 months after seeing a Nativity play at Christmas time. Poppy's wish to be her mother's only baby, a special Jesus-like baby, was confirmed by mother.

In this short piece of work it was not possible to explore Mrs Green's relationship with her mother, apart from the rare hints she made. The miscarriage had occurred during a visit of her mother, who was living in a distant part of the British Isles. After another visit of her mother and sister for a few days, Mrs Green expressed relief when they left. An ambivalent relationship with the members of her family of origin seemed still to persist and to influence Mrs Green's feelings and approach to life.

My hypothesis, which was confirmed by Mrs Green, was that the unborn baby had not been mourned by her but had been replaced by either a regression to a baby state in Poppy, or by a continuation of Poppy's non-separate baby state. The unmourned loss (Pozzi, 1993, p. 139) had probably reactivated past losses which had not been dealt with and had left Mrs Green feeling depressed, deflated, tired and unable to handle Poppy's tyrannical control and difficulties at separating from mother. A collusive dynamic between mother and child had set in, thus hindering the chances of moving on. Mrs Green could not have another baby and Poppy could not move out of 'being a baby'.

Father eventually came unexpectedly to the clinic one day. My original letter had invited both parents to attend the sessions but he had not been able to come. At first he acted as if supervising my work with his wife and Poppy, then he became more involved. Some anxieties about Poppy dying were shared by both parents – who disagreed on many other issues related to rearing their child. The issue of death had to do with a dangerous river in their garden, which, in their minds, posed a threat to Poppy's life. However, their attitude was rather unrealistic and the river seemed to provide them with an external reason for them to express deeper conflicts and anxieties. Poppy was so shy that she would never have ventured as far as that river and nothing had ever been done to fence the river off on that side of their garden. Mother and father seemed to collude in the idea that being out of sight and separate were equated with dying.

Mother's heavy depression, which also clouded my mind during the sessions, lifted in part through our work. However, her feeling of only having 'limited resources', as the T-shirt Mrs Green once wore read, only allowed 'limited achievements' in letting go of Poppy very slowly.

Children at risk: disturbed adults to be. Links with Narcissus's vicissitudes

The risk for Peter and Poppy – had they not received any help – and for all the children whose mothers' needs come first, is that their emotional growth could be severely impaired. They get stuck at the phase of separation and individuation, and narcissistic disturbances are likely to emerge as well as problems in the area of sexual identity and of internalisation and identification with aspects of their parents.

Peter may have grown into a confused and disturbed adult with possible difficulties in his sexual identity. He may have resorted to 'becoming a woman', the mother, in his wish to be a girl – as he had expressed – and as a desperate attempt to have his mother, had he not been helped to internalise her and separate from her.

Poppy's omnipotent phantasies of controlling her object, of having destroyed the rivalrous siblings and children, and of being the only survivor were partially dealt with in the short therapy. However, she may still develop into an insecure and yet tyrannical personality impaired in her emotional development and life.

The omnipotent, controlling and tyrannical phantasies of children are part of normal development but need to be transformed by the parental figures and reintrojected by the child in more real terms, so that adaptation to reality can be achieved through the acceptance of psychic pain. However, if the parent is either stuck and unable to face the pain of being different and separate from the child, or to challenge the child's omnipotent phantasies of power and control, then the perpetuation of fragile, insecure, narcissistic personalities will be fostered.

In the cases described here it is noticeable that the paternal figure is often absent, not strong enough or not asked for help by the mother to handle her narcissistic involvement with her child and her lack of separateness. The Oedipal triangulation is lacking in these families or is reversed so that it is the child who ends up performing the function of a spouse to the needy parent, thus becoming the recipient of parental needs, difficulties and phantasies.

We are reminded of Narcissus's vicissitudes. Mollon (1993, p. 33) writes:

> The origins of Narcissus are violent – a violent 'primal scene' as the nymph Liriope is raped by the river god Cephisus. There is no continuing parental couple and no father available to Narcissus. Narcissus's origins are preceded by the pronouncement that he should not know himself . . . Narcissus becomes trapped in his incapacity to recognise himself . . . . Violence, envy, sadism and masochism pervade the story, which is one of repeated victimisation. Narcissus treats Echo and his other admirers sadistically . . . On the other hand, masochism is represented in Echo's enslavement to Narcissus, her inability to take any initiative in the 'dialogue', her entrapment in a position of passive response to Narcissus.

Victoria Hamilton (1982) sees Echo and Narcissus as fitting together perfectly and as mutually trapped in a 'mirroring or doting symbiosis which resists change'.

Thinking of the mother-and-child relationships already illustrated, the links with Narcissus's story become clear. Mrs Green and Mrs Smith appeared trapped in a doting symbiosis with their idealised children as well as in tyrannical mutual control of a sadomasochistic nature.

Links between mourning, separation and narcissism

Here I explore the link between maternal separation difficulties, the process of mourning and narcissistic traits in the mother's personality.

Freud (1917, p. 243) compares the condition of melancholia with that of mourning. He writes that in both conditions the reaction to the loss of someone who is loved – and also of 'some abstraction' such as one's country, liberty, an ideal and so on – produces similar responses. These are a painful sense of dejection, a loss of interest in the outside world or an interest only in what recalls the lost object, the loss of the capacity to find another object of love, the inhibition of all activity, although in mourning activities are exclusively related to the lost object.

He also addresses the question of what the work of mourning consists of:

> Reality-testing has shown that the love object no longer exists, and it proceeds to demand that all libido shall be withdrawn from attachment to that object. . . . Normally respect for reality gains the day . . . [When] the work of mourning is completed the ego becomes free and uninhibited again.

However, in melancholia the free libido was not:

... displayed onto another object; it was withdrawn into the ego. [It] served to establish an *identification* of the ego with the abandoned object. Thus the shadow of the object fell upon the ego ... As Otto Rank has aptly remarked, . . . the object-choice has been effected on a narcissistic basis, so that the object-cathexis, when obstacles come in its way, can regress to narcissism.

Freud (1917, pp. 244–5, 249)

Freud reflected on the idea that 'the disposition to fall ill of melancholia ... lies in the predominance of the narcissistic type of object-choice' (p. 250).

In thinking of Mrs Smith and Mrs Green, they were both suffering from depression – a mild form of melancholia – although neither of them was aware of their depression. The deadly sessions with Mrs Green, in which my thinking could barely survive (Pozzi, 1993), and the deadness in Mrs Smith's and Peter's eyes, as well as her anger towards him, had alerted me to thinking that neither mothers had managed to work through their recent and past losses. Following Freud and Otto Rank's ideas we can infer that narcissistic traits were rather strong in both women and had held back the resolution of their mourning, i.e. their capacity to separate from and let go of their lost children and to invest in new objects of love. Instead they projectively identified with their toddlers, i.e. treated them as substitutes of the lost objects. It seems to me that something must have gone wrong in these mothers' own childhood and in their relationships with their parents. Mrs Green and Mrs Smith's internal world had not been sufficiently modified for them to be able to break – with their small children – the circle of unresolved loss.

The child as a vessel of parental projections

Both mothers described were well-meaning and reasonably well-adjusted personalities on the whole, and had not suffered from major psychological traumas, abuses, etc. However, something had gone wrong in specific areas of their emotional lives, which gave rise to the difficulties described with their children. Erna Furman (1994) explores some of the reasons for the difficulties that mothers encounter on being left by their children. She refers to the various kinds of narcissistic wounds mothers experience when faced with either the loss of a child by death or the loss of a developmental phase of the child growing up. The mothers described in this chapter had great difficulties in separating from their children and could not mourn the death of the previous baby or the miscarried baby. In baby observations (Bick, 1968), the relationship between mother and baby is followed from its early days and possible later disturbances may be seen in their embryonic form. Two dreams from an observation of a pregnant mother with narcissistic disposition revealed that her baby was unconsciously experienced as an intrusion into a self-sufficient, narcissistic couple. The baby turned into a broach to embellish mother in the first dream, while in the second the baby was seen as a dangerous and messy instinctual being who was being abandoned to death by freezing. In the following 2 years of weekly observations it was noted that this maternal streak did affect the baby's development.

In following Klein (1952), Rosenfeld tried to understand the nature of narcissism and emphasised that it was not an objectless state. Therefore he introduced the term 'narcissistic object-relation' to describe the particular relationship that some patients (he refers mainly to psychotic ones) have with their objects. It is a relationship based on narcissistic purposes and on omnipotence (Rosenfeld, 1987, p. 20). He wrote that 'many conditions that resembled Freud's description of primary narcissism are in fact primary object-relations' (Rosenfeld, 1964, p. 170). He thought that narcissism is a defence against separateness which is denied via the mechanism of projective identification. According to Kleinian and post-Kleinian authors and clinicians, in projective identification unwanted parts of oneself are split and projected into an object, i.e. a person who is then seen as possessing those aspects of the self and as being modified by such projections. Rosenfeld (1987, pp. 20–1) thought that the patient simultaneously 'identifies . . . with the object to the extent that he feels he is the object or the object is himself. . . . The object becomes part of the self to such a degree that any separate identity or boundary between self and object is felt not to exist'. The self and the object appear to be the same. In this state of sameness, feelings lose their virulence or are not felt at all. If two people are felt to be the same, there is no comparison, competition, envy, anger, frustration, but a flat so-called equality.

In the cases discussed here, first of all we notice a reverse of the projective identification, i.e. it is the mother, and not the child, who projects into the baby or the child something unbearable, e.g. the anxieties about separation and separateness. The child's needs and feelings are not seen as different from the mother's; the child is a narcissistic extension of the parent's needs and desires, and is not treated as a separate person in his or her own right. In Mrs Smith's case, due to unbearable pain, the death of her baby was not mourned properly. She related to Peter as if he were a living image of the dead baby. Mother's separation difficulties paralysed her relationship with Poppy in Mrs Green's case.

In this form of reversal, however, the child cannot contain – contain in Bion's terms – the parental projections, but is bombarded and shuttered by such projections. That is why I prefer to use the word 'vessel' to describe the parent's unconscious use of the child and this is very different from the function of container. The objects of such maternal projective identifications, i.e. the children, were no longer perceived as separate people but as vessels of mother's anxieties. Frustrations, pain and depression were thus in part avoided by these mothers and some relief from anxiety was gained at the expense of these children's development. They were somehow forced to enact a role and a function desired by their mothers. Peter had no identity of his own but had become some version of his dead baby brother; Poppy could not let go of mother but stuck to her and buffered her from separation anxiety. The mother's ego had become weaker because of the loss of those parts split and projected into the child. These mothers became dependent on their children for their own happiness and survival, thus perpetuating the reversal of a relationship of dependency of the child on the mother. Children who are subjected to this fate are likely to grow into adults with more or less severe identity and personality problems depending on both the severity of the parental projective identification and the child's own inner character structure and other factors.

The therapeutic intervention with these two mothers may have increased the awareness of the deep processes going on in the relationships between them, their children and husbands and hopefully helped enough for some modification to occur.

References

Bick E (1964). Notes on infant observation in psychoanalytic training. *International Journal of Psycho-Analysis* 45: 558–66.

Bick E (1968). The experience of the skin in early object relations. *International Journal of Psycho-Analysis* 49: 484–6.

Bion WR (1963). *Elements of Psycho-Analysis*. London: Maresfield Reprints.

Freud S (1917). Mourning and melancholia. *The Complete Psychological Works of Sigmund Freud*, standard edition, vol. 14, pp. 237–58. London: Hogarth Press.

Furman E (1994). Early aspects of mothering: What makes it so hard to be there to be left. *Journal of Child Psychotherapy* 20 (2): 149–64.

Hamilton V (1982). *Narcissism and Oedipus*. London: Routledge & Kegan Paul.

Klein M (1952). *Envy and Gratitude*. New York: A Delta Book. Reprinted 1975.

Mollon P (1993). *The Fragile Self*. London: Whurr Publishers.

Pozzi ME (1993). It is never the right time: how to help a mother separate from her young child. *Psychoanalytic Psychotherapy* 7(2): 135–47.

Rosenfeld HA (1964). On the psychopathology of narcissism: a clinical approach. *Psychotic States*. London: Maresfield Reprints.

Rosenfeld HA (1987). *Impasse and Interpretation*. London, New York: Tavistock.

Chapter 4
Narcissistic vulnerability in adolescence

SARA FLANDERS

Conveying the sharp mix of newly wakened vivacity and a reciprocal mournfulness associated with the loss of childhood, Virginia Woolf describes the mood swings of her adolescent hero in *Jacob's Room*. He relishes the muscular independence, the sensual risks in sailing and swimming together with a friend, but still looks with sorrow at the houses on the Cornish hills:

> . . . the chimneys and the coastguard stations and the little bays with the waves breaking unseen by anyone make one remember the overpowering sorrow. And what can this sorrow be?
> It is brewed by the earth itself. It comes from the houses on the coast. We start transparent, and then the cloud thickens. All history backs our pane of glass.
>
> *Woolf (1922)*

All history, from the earliest experiences in the emotional and physical intimacy of the relationship with the mother, colours the experience of the self, the body, the desires and their object. Virginia Woolf betrays, in the preference for transparency, her own struggle with the realities of the body, the thickened cloud of physicality that she presents in this book, unusually for her, as homely, benign and potentially good. In the character of Jacob's mother, she offers the most poignant portrayal she would ever achieve of a 'good enough' mother – that requirement, as Winnicott (1958, 1965, 1971) did not tire of reminding us, which provides the foundations for the inevitable losses associated with maturation, the secure base (Bowlby, 1988) from which it will become safe enough eventually to push off. Like Jacob – not like Virginia Woolf herself, whose first novel *The Voyage Out* catalogues a disastrous entry into adulthood which more accurately reflects her own experience – the best way to separate from the protected haven of childhood is with a sense of self, a toleration of loss, a capacity to love, a relationship to reality which includes the adult sexual body. A tall order, and a task that takes the better part of a decade to accomplish.

40

Whether it has been awaited with excitement and hope or arrives as an intolerable, terrifying invasion, puberty is intrusive, outside the child's conscious control. The mysterious otherness of adulthood discloses itself from inside out, through the contours of the body, and in the specificity of sexual maturity, the new realities of masculinity and femininity, the functions of ejaculation and menstruation, the substances of semen and blood. Adolescents will interpret the changes which take place in their bodies at puberty through the lens that they have developed, the capacities for emotional and sensual experience that are the product of their development.

By their very nature, these changes challenge the sense of identity and well-being, the narcissistic equilibrium of the grown-up child, even as the fact of the physical growth of the increasingly adult young man or woman potentially rewards self-regard, the benign heritage of infantile narcissism (Freud, 1914). A process full of the new, adolescence reawakens archaic and disturbing excitements and anxieties, requires risk and produces failures, disappointments, experiences of shame along with the discovery of now realisable joy and mastery. Such stuff of emotional growth, of learning, is only bearable if the adolescent brings to the project a capacity to bear the exhilarating but alarming range of feelings appropriate to the normal process. Yet it is the very inability to bear intensified emotions of shame (Kohut, 1971) along with an envious intolerance of loss (Klein, 1957; Rosenfeld, 1964, 1971) which have come to be regarded as the hallmarks of the narcissistically vulnerable personality. The impact of adolescent sexual development will therefore bring particular disturbance for the narcissistically vulnerable. And for the most fragile, those for whom any sense of self is precariously held in rigid, idealised identifications, change brings disaster, fragmentation, breakdown. This is the psychotic end of the spectrum of narcissistic disturbance and the nature of adolescence is to provoke it.

Narcissism and sexuality: Freud

In 1905, Freud explained, in 'The sexual enlightenment of children', that the adult sexuality normally and correctly identified with the awakening of puberty is in fact a reawakening. The sexual drives have been active since birth and travelled a complex path before settling, after the passionate upheaval of the Oedipus, into the 'latency' stage which is then in turn so definitively and permanently disturbed by the advent of sexual adulthood. By 1914 he understood the complex history of the sexual drive to be crucially entwined with the fate of the child's 'original narcissism', the eventual and necessary dethronement of 'His majesty the baby' (Freud, 1914). The developmental conceptualisation of 'Narcissism: an introduction' grew out of consideration first of homosexual object choice (Freud, 1905, 1910) and then in relation to the megalomania, or profoundly inflated and delusional self-love, of the psychotic (Freud, 1911). In both cases, the demands of a precarious narcissistic equilibrium pull the subject away: in homosexuality from the otherness of the opposite sex and, more extremely, in psychosis, away from reality itself. Transient homosexual and psychotic functioning frequently mark the stormier adolescent passage, and signify intense conflict in meeting the demands of integrating the reality which includes the changed body (Laufer and Laufer, 1984).

Narcissism and sexuality: post-Freud

Since the time of Freud's pioneering work on narcissism and the deepening enquiry of Freud and his colleagues into early infantile experience, more is understood of the way in which the first months and years of the child's life contribute to the development of the strengths, the sense of personal continuity and worth which enables the child to bear the anxieties of separateness and the vicissitudes of desire (Winnicott, 1958, 1965, 1971; Mahler and Furer, 1968; Stern, 1985). If early experiences of separation or, indeed, of intimacy are too enraging or terrifying, then individuality and intimate communication are coloured too intensely with emotional experiences of abandonment or violent intrusion or engulfment (Green, 1975; Glasser, 1979) and the renewed separation of adolescence will be correspondingly anguished. Whatever the early experience, the loss of childhood involves a real diminishing of the protection of parents, whose magic decreases as the powers of the adolescent increase along with the demands of adult life. Strongly held illusions regarding the child's specialness are radically challenged. These illusions have modified the envy, jealousy and disappointments of childhood, and frequently been erected as bulwarks against the awareness of the shaming, largely unconscious memories of infantile instinctual life (Grunberger, 1979). The more rigid and defensive this idealisation of childhood, which is, after all, a powerful feature of much parental love (Freud, 1914), the more intrusive and disturbing the beginning of adult sexual life (Laufer and Laufer, 1984). The narcissistically most vulnerable adolescent brings the most powerful resistances to the loss of an idealised status which is inevitably shattered by the changes that take place within the destabilised boundaries of the body itself.

Adolescence will therefore reawaken old narcissistic injuries, and will challenge defensive denials erected to protect a fragile self-esteem or, *in extremis*, the very coherence of a fragile identity. What sense did the Oedipal child make of the parents' exclusive sexuality, assuming that the child's boundaries were not assaulted by sexual abuse, which would provoke specific vulnerability? Confrontation with the fact of exclusion from the parents' sexual relation to each other needs to have been bearable to the Oedipal child. Self-esteem needs to have survived the encounter between adult reality and childhood ambitions, so that the sexual reality that develops at adolescence will not be too hateful. If the parents' relationship is too cruelly or hatefully conceived, it is likely that the hatred will permeate and pervert the adolescent's relation to his own body and that of his object. Brittle rigidities which have resulted from loss experienced as too traumatic, separation too frightening, strong feelings too disturbing, sexuality too intrusive or violent or dirty (Grunberger, 1979) will leave the adolescent poorly equipped to face up to the challenges of his new opportunity and defensively estranged from sexual realities.

The sexually mature body

The mature body which has heralded the loss of childhood and the advent of adult sexuality frequently becomes then the object of strategies aimed to control the panic associated with new and frightening development. Hated sexual feelings find expression and are simultaneously defended against in symptoms that aim to put an end to the living reality of desires that are not supportable, are incompatible with the fragile adolescent's sense of worth or well-being. The body which is interpreted to have betrayed the self, exposed the self to the abandonment of parental protection, lost forever some idealised, often purified, sense of specialness becomes an object of attack. Strategies such as anorexia, bulimia, self-inflicted injury, attempted suicide are familiar to anyone who has much contact with disturbed adolescents. All such activities argue a breakdown in the adolescent's struggle to integrate the reality as he or she perceives it, of the body which has matured into an adult sexual body, masculine or feminine, differentiated, individual (Laufer and Laufer, 1984).

The narcissistically vulnerable adolescent feels compelled to repudiate or magically control his or her development, and can be driven by such a compulsion further and further from reality, finally to the most radically omnipotent act of suicide itself. When an adolescent is in this much trouble, he or she is in need of therapeutic help which might begin to sponsor an ability to bear the desperately hated, narcissistically humiliating emotional life always linked in adolescence to the newness of sexual maturity (Laufer and Laufer, 1984).

All adolescents put up with painfully demanding volatility, disappointments born of the risks that are the adolescent's task to undertake. Frequently the group is able to help take care of the new adolescent loneliness, provide balm for the narcissistic sensitivities which are always alive, provide comforting reassurance to the feelings of alienation and exposure produced by the newness of young adulthood. For the most vulnerable, such solace is unavailable; the severity of their difficulties truly places them outside the limits of what a group can carry. Their risks lead to failures which are experienced as a desperate and total internal and external abandonment. Theirs is a sense of worthlessness which inspires the suicidal thoughts, plans, actions, which are a feature of troubled adolescence.

Clinical example

An adolescent, whom I shall call Mary, sought treatment after returning home from boarding school and complained of feeling 'not right', an opaque and barely communicative statement which was designed to express and cover at the same time a disturbance so frightening to this girl that she allowed herself only the narrowest range of feeling, the most minimal awareness of her emotional life. The narcissistic flavour of her complaint nevertheless makes itself felt in the language of imperfection through which she gave voice to her difficulty, bringing to mind nothing so much as a flawed product on the conveyer belt of normality. This deadened, minimalist language was one aspect of the rigidity, the determined control which held this young woman together in a pious, saintly seeming silence, inarticulacy being one of her complaints. She had nothing to say, she could not 'join in'; she came to therapy to find a way to 'join in' which meant, among other things, to have the feelings that she deemed to be bearable and good, a limited, superficial notion that nevertheless held out her only hope.

Inevitably the 'normality' she sought would be coloured by the rigid idealisations of her narcissism. She certainly did not come to explore her own feelings, a project quite contrary to the desperate foreclosure of her own emotional life. Rather, she entered therapy with a specifically narcissistic project, a search for the resurrection of an ideal self, identified as normal, but not truly conceived as emotionally alive or sexually engaged. This aliveness, valued by any therapist, held too much terror for this 18-year-old. In such a situation, it is left to the therapist to hold this potential in mind on behalf of the adolescent who is so keen to achieve normality, but whose experience of emotionality is so associated with what is bad that normality is precisely what is, as Freud and Breuer noted so long ago, 'strangulated' out of existence (Freud, 1895).

In addition to the longing to fit in, the dread of abnormality and an intolerance of strong feeling which plunged her easily and regularly into suicidal despair, she complained of a severe and frightening eating disorder. Unwanted and unattended feelings found expression through the bulimic bingeing and vomiting into which she would pour her raw and disowned feelings, her rage and her hated desires. With the vomiting, she gained the control over the lifeless object, the food, with which she filled herself, then rid herself of. A vicious circle, however, had been established. She felt, after such a session, not only temporarily stabilised, but also hopelessly despairing and bad, even further away from the idealised, neutralised normality to which she aspired, and also, as she was only too well aware, further away from any ordinary relationship. The rigid, dehumanised idealisations which guided this vulnerable adolescent demanded too much of her, and so led her into paroxysms of humiliated self-loathing, the state of mind that followed a binge. But the symptom, which aimed to restore some sense of omnipotence over overwhelming anxiety, was not easily given up, itself a manifestation of the starved liveliness this young girl did not quite manage to stifle completely.

The eating disorder developed when, at the age of 16, she found herself in a relationship with a boy who belonged to the family she and her mother were visiting in the country of the mother's origin. Only after her first intercourse, as is often the case, did the compulsive eating start. She associated the symptom not with the boyfriend or the intercourse, but with a simultaneous relationship with the boy's mother, a friend of her own mother, who with excessive hospitable zeal pressed food on her to which she felt she could not say 'no'. Whatever the truth of the historical memory, it expresses a paranoid and helpless state before a maternal figure who stuffs her and tries to control her, filling her up, as it happens in this case, with good food which she imagined would make her fat and undesirable. This preoccupation and the repetition, within her omnipotence, of the stuffing in the bingeing and vomiting, displaced and subsumed most of the feeling she brought at 18 of the memory of a sexual relationship. The vicissitudes of sexual involvement yielded to the reawakened desires associated with the profoundly problematic relationship to the mother, the foundation of her disturbed sense of self, difference and desire, her narcissistic vulnerability.

Indeed, the loss of the boyfriend represented less a loss of a sexual relationship and much more acutely a narcissistic injury which left Mary deflated, depressed, hopeless, suicidal, in despair of the blessed normality that having a boyfriend signified. Inasmuch as this relationship came alive at all in treatment, it seemed primarily associated with salvation and rescue from worthlessness and abnormality, and was otherwise dominated by an anxious terror of not 'fitting in', being unlike the others, the boyfriend's group, in which she had momentarily taken her place. No reference to the reality of sexual intimacy was ever spontaneously disclosed, and it seems that probably she was quite disassociated from it, although I never doubted its existence.

Within the relationship, as she described it, she had felt above all unable to initiate a communication of her own, in intimacy or within the group. She could not speak, could not 'break the ice'. Her language, impassively clichéd, illustrates truly the frozen impasse in which this girl was stuck. Such inhibition is a product of this young woman's great difficulty in experiencing her separateness, her uniqueness, her difference as anything but a terrifying exposure to the void of potential abandonment.

Finding no fulfilment in the possibility of individuality and sexual difference and articulate speech – she could not say 'no' – she returned in her
preoccupations to the relationship at the heart of her vulnerability, bind-
ing herself to the circularity of the bingeing and vomiting cycle, a
perverse, dehumanised parody of the earliest form of gratification. This
cycle circumscribed her narcissistic entrapment, her defensive withdrawal from the vicissitudes of intimacy, emotional life, relationship. It is
confirmation of an inability to separate from her primary object, and a
product of her unreadiness for the sexual relationship that she misguid-
edly but hopefully had embarked on. All her lively feelings and excitements were then re-engaged in the primitive struggle with a maternal
object with whom and to whom she remained both helplessly and deter-
minedly stuck. A realistic terror of remaining locked forever in the
dreaded but also longed for claustrophobic situation with her mother
had become the preoccupying fear that drove her into treatment.

The narcissistic transference: breaking the ice

Part of the paralysing intolerance of any emotionality can be understood
as the danger to herself in this regressed emotional situation. It partially
explains the most notable feature in the first period of therapy which
was the uncanny, pious solemnity of her profoundly quietistic presence.
I either worked very hard on very little material or struggled with deadened feelings bordering on sleep. I understand this now as a manifestation of her extreme fear of the encounter with me, anticipating my
otherness as fundamentally dangerous unless she could in some way 'fit
in' with my preconceptions, my projections. She successfully controlled
our meetings and me, as I laboured to produce the interpretations with
which she was then presented as with too much food. Anything new that
I tried to bring to understanding her internal situation she experienced
as a reproach, not new information but the thing that she should have
been thinking in order to be a perfect reproduction of me, to keep the
gap closed between us. Occasionally, and quite alarmingly in the early
encounters, she looked as if she was having to swallow regurgitated
food, and my assumption was that I was almost literally forcing indi-
gestible material into her. With excessive care, too mindful of Mary's
dread of contact, the blame with which she experienced any observation
different from her own, I managed to provide, from time to time, a
manageable surprise, avoiding at the same time too much disturbance of
precarious equilibrium.

Gradually Mary did develop some minimal sense of safety in the therapeutic situation. I would not exaggerate the freedom achieved; she in no
way became curious enough about her mind and its processes to bring,
for example, dreams, except on a rare occasion near the end of the therapy. She did, however, become eager to speak of life and face some of her

conflicts and some of the realities, including her determined dependence on a disturbed mother. She managed to recognise her adhesive attachment to paranoid processes which she used passively to avoid the burden and fear of her own thoughts and feelings.

A first problem for Mary then was the fact of her own mother's susceptibility to mental disturbance. I believe, on the basis of known history and transference phenomena, that Mary's rigid control, her lack of trust in boundaries between her and me, her deep sense of danger and lack of faith in the communicative, symbolic processes were a product of having been consistently, from infancy, exposed to intermittent psychotic intrusion. She was left with powerful defences which she no doubt projected into the therapeutic consistencies, and so was able, in her way, to use psychotherapy precisely to resurrect the narcissistic ideal she held on to for dear life. I inherited her own rigid capacities to hold herself together, a fundamental project of the narcissistic personality. In as much as the constancy of the psychotherapeutic situation fulfilled the rigidities of the ego development so manifest in Mary's personality, she trusted it, clung to it, however long she took to be able to use it (Winnicott, 1971). Such rigidities and such profoundly controlling demands on her own emotionality leave one in no doubt of the enormous strain the upheavals of the adolescent process placed on her, and the hopeless strains placed on her first sexual relationship.

Refinding the father

The history was complicated not only by the accumulated trauma of disturbed maternal thought processes, paranoid mentation which disclosed itself frequently through Mary's own retreat into them, as well as through the bizarre activities actually reported. Mary's childhood was also marked by traumatic life events, which served to lock her into fixations, and into complex terrors associated with her own drives and those with which she identified. Most significantly a violent separation between her parents when she was a 4-year-old child saw her father escorted by police away from the home. He and his daughter met rarely thereafter, and Mary was left to form a passionate and exclusive relationship with her mother until she was sent to boarding school following her mother's liaison with a second husband. The narcissistic threats of engulfment and abandonment, at the Oedipal and then at the pubertal milestones, intruded into this girl's life through the first marital separation which was accompanied by actual violence, and in the second, which she experienced as abandonment by the mother. The first subverted her emotional growth, provoking enforced closeness at the age when she would be most in need of some benign acceptance of distance and confusing the project of identification with the mother with a real experience of replacing the father. She was traumatised in reverse at puberty when the mother turned to an adult male partner whom Mary regarded as a hated, greedy usurper, entirely on the model of a rival child. The battle between the possessive child and the intruding adult male was superficially solved by sending the protesting girl to boarding school. She was left with passionate homosexual longings for the mother she had in phantasy partnered for the duration of her latency years. This primitive attachment was the most shaming and anxiety-provoking pull in her emotional life, another strong emotional current to be dammed up and rigidly controlled.

Added to the sense of injury, the furious jealousy, the enormous difficulty in tolerating loss, the boarding school placement, which may well have saved this girl from a nightmarish adolescence at home, sealed her I believe in a frozen narcissistic bleakness. The susceptibility to suicidal thoughts followed the onset of puberty which carried, in this circumstance so vividly, the added meaning of banishment and humiliation and loss of the maternal attachment which was intense and sexualised. During these early adolescent years this girl was supported primarily by the hope of receiving therapy when she left boarding school, which hope was supported by infrequent but regular contact with a therapeutic agency. This hope was crucial to her fragile mental survival, although it did carry with it the burden of the rigid idealisation, the characteristic style of self-holding that sustained her.

In the course of her therapy, a longing to be in touch with a father who, in her mind, might come between her and the regressive potential of her relationship to her mother materialised in a real search for her father. In fact, contact with her real father reproduced the disappointing, ineffectual contact of the past. However, in thinking about and searching for and mourning the loss of her father she was able to establish some significant paternal meaningfulness within her internal world, and this development was crucial to whatever growth her therapy was able to facilitate. Simply by validating the importance of the father, I was able to make a useful intervention into the regressive, mother–daughter stasis. Moreover, her two therapy sessions per week no doubt reproduced the alternative, paternally created space which allowed this girl some chance to find her separate voice and to identify her own desire. How much of this function was actually internalised symbolically was not clear in the therapy. Caution is validated by the fact that she was never happily able to spend more than two evenings per week with the boyfriend she met while in twice-weekly therapy.

With narcissistic difficulties etched so deeply into the character of this girl who grew up in an emotionally unreliable though consciously concerned and perhaps even devoted context, it is remarkable that she was able to use therapy to facilitate some significant individual growth, and enjoy some of the pleasures and achievements appropriate to young adulthood. A daunting and potentially strangulating perfectionism released its grip on her capacity to bear the vicissitudes of ordinary discourse sufficiently for her to reap the benefits of her consistent precision at work. This corresponded to a modest shift in willingness to explore feelings, to tolerate doubt, to acknowledge her confusion, to disclose some spontaneity, even to say 'no' to me. Indeed, the extent to which she became able to differ with me marked the beginning of a differentiation process that also included the tentative awareness of her own mother's paranoia. She was able to establish a relationship with a boyfriend and have a sexual involvement which included sometimes a capacity for emotional closeness and communication. She was aware of how intermittent this was, how much she struggled either with an emotional state of withdrawn, silent bleakness, or furious jealousy, or enslaved submissiveness. When, however, she was able to communicate with her boyfriend and make herself understood, she was enormously relieved and then refrained for some time from bingeing and vomiting. Roughly, these achievements corresponded to her ability to be alive with me, to have in the transference an alive but not volatile intrusive object.

It is interesting that where the truest growth in this treatment seemed to take place was in the last year of a 3-year time-limited treatment. As the limit made itself felt and impinged on the illusion of timelessness, i.e. on the omnipotent phantasy of a permanent alliance with me, the idea of a potentially beneficial separateness, even a life-giving one, awakened a sense of good urgency as opposed to panic. One might hypothesise and, indeed, I did at the time, that this limit functioned again as the paternal signifier, reinforcing the boundaries between therapist and patient in a necessary, facilitating way. This might be particularly significant in the adolescent's therapy, in which the regressive pull is always so powerful and often such a threat to any committed treatment. There is no doubt in my mind that this period was markedly more emotionally alive. However, it would also have to be said that panic did reassert itself as the ending proved, as it became imminent, to be finally inconceivable. It was not worked through. With the firm splitting mechanisms on which idealisation so profoundly depends, this now young woman managed to make use of the limit, but not to link it with the actuality of a projected ending of therapy. That is to say, the good limit of the institutionalised therapy which on some level represented a paternal interference with powerful maternal omnipotence, actually became, as it came nearer to the ending, an attack on her own narcissistic omnipotence, to which she clung, precisely as the ending pressed on her. The end of treatment then actualised and repeated the unthinkable trauma, reinvoked narcissistic defences, and this in spite of many interpretations of the anxiety and fury associated with ending.

However much the adolescent process was facilitated by this therapy, and this young woman took some large steps into adulthood, the profundities of the mental mechanisms by which her development had been distorted have not relinquished the threat to the next steps in her life, which she is, however, in a better place to take. She knows something of the experience of being helped and will, I believe, seek it for herself in the future.

References

Bowlby J (1988). *A Secure Base: Clinical Applications of Attachment Theory*. London: Routledge.

Freud S (1895). Studies on hysteria. *The Complete Psychological Works of Sigmund Freud*, standard edition, vol. 2. London: Hogarth Press, 1955.

Freud S (1905). Three essays on the theory of sexuality. *The Complete Psychological Works of Sigmund Freud*, standard edition, vol. 8. London: Hogarth Press.

Freud S (1910). Leonardo da Vinci and a memory of his childhood. *The Complete Psychological Works of Sigmund Freud*, standard edition, vol. 11. London: Hogarth Press.

Freud S (1911). Psychoanalytic notes on an autobiographical account of a case of paranoia. *The Complete Psychological Works of Sigmund Freud*, standard edition, vol. 12. London: Hogarth Press.

Freud S (1914). On narcissism: An introduction. *The Complete Psychological Works of Sigmund Freud*, standard edition, vol. 14. London: Hogarth Press.

Glasser M (1979). Some aspects of the role of aggression in the perversions. In I Rosen (Ed.), *Sexual Deviations*. Oxford: Oxford University Press.

Green A (1975). The analyst, symbolization and absence in the analytic setting. *International Journal of Psycho-Analysis* 56: 1–19.

Grunberger B (1979). *Narcissism*. Madison, CT: International Universities Press.

Klein M (1957). *Envy and gratitude*. In The Writings of Melanie Klein, vol. 3, *Envy and Gratitude and Other Works*. London: Hogarth Press.

Kohut H (1971). *The Analysis of the Self*. New York: International Universities Press.

Laplanche J, Pontalis J (1983). *The Language of Psychoanalysis*. London: Hogarth Press.

Laufer M, Laufer M E (1984). *Adolescence and Developmental Breakdown*. New Haven, London: Yale.

Mahler M, Furer M (1968). *On Human Symbiosis and the Vicissitudes of Individuation*. New York: International Universities Press.

Rosenfeld H (1964). On the psychopathology of narcissism: a clinical approach. *International Journal of Psycho-Analysis* 45: 332–7.

Rosenfeld H (1971). A clinical approach to the psychoanalytic theory of the life and death instincts: An investigation into the aggressive aspects of narcissism. *International Journal of Psycho-Analysis* 52: 169–78.

Stern D (1985). *The Interpersonal World of the Infant*. New York: Basic Books.

Winnicott DW (1958). *Through Paediatrics to Psychoanalysis*. London: Hogarth Press, 1982.

Winnicott DW (1965). *The Maturational Processes and the Facilitating Environment*. London: Hogarth Press.

Winnicott DW (1971). *Playing and Reality*. London: Tavistock Press.

Woolf V (1915). *The Voyage Out*. London: Duckworth.

Woolf V (1922). *Jacob's Room*. London: Hogarth Press; Oxford: Oxford University Press, 1992.

Chapter 5
Narcissism and adolescence

PETER WILSON

It can be no surprise that adolescents are peculiarly bothered about themselves. There is a great deal going on. The fundamental pubertal changes, combined with expanding cognitive capacities, create an unprecedented state in the life of the individual. The adolescent lives in a state of new physical tension, with sharpened awareness and broader understanding. These changes occur in the context of shifting patterns and alliances within the family and in relation to a demand both from within and from outside the family to achieve independence, find work, and take on adult and parental responsibilities. In the midst of all this, preoccupations with self-value and self-coherence are inevitable.

The adolescent predicament

There is by definition no stability in adolescence. The adolescent is in a constant process of adjustment and transition, contending with new unexpected sensations and fantasies, and struggling to find a place in the outside world – with siblings and parents and with other people in the community beyond. The sheer pressure of the developmental and maturational advances of adolescence is such as to give rise to considerable anxiety. There is the fear of the loss of childhood dependency and familiarity, a growing uneasy sense of alienation and aloneness. The gradual questioning of the implicit belief in parental protectiveness (however illusory) adds to this fear. There is the uncertainty about the challenge and demands that lie ahead and doubts about adequacy, success and the capacity to survive by oneself. There is anxiety too, given the increase of sexual and aggressive potential and the loss of earlier equilibrium and containment, that things will get out of hand – that there will be a failure to contain impulses or hold things together. There is above all in adolescence a particular terror of limitlessness – of there being no bounds to possibility, no end to what might happen or be found out.

These anxieties constitute the core of adolescent experience; they give rise to a specific kind of developmental vulnerability that is characteristic of this period of life. It is of vital concern to adolescents to hold on to a measure of self-control and to gain a sense of themselves that encompasses the new diversity of experience and opportunity. The central focus in the fray of all the buffeting is to draw together the various aspects of this experience and achieve some kind of self-integration and definition. Adolescence is thus a time when narcissistic preoccupations prevail. Perhaps more than in any other period of life, the overriding and compelling concern is with the nature of the self and its continuity, and with the search for integrity and worth. The questions that nag and persist, against a constant background of change and uncertainty, are familiar: 'Who am I?', 'What am I?', 'What am I for?' and 'Am I the same as I was yesterday?' These are private questions, integral to the process of individuation and separation and to adolescents' realisation that they must find and take responsibility for themselves (just as they must care for and take ownership of their own bodies). In achieving this, adolescents need to distance themselves from their parents and care takers; the emotional investment that they once placed in parents as children has to be withdrawn and directed more exclusively towards themselves (Blos, 1962).

There is in fact a very distinctive insularity in the adolescent experience and a keen, almost overwhelming, sense of its fragility. Adolescents exist in a disturbing vacuum, created by the growing detachment from their parents. They are aware, at different levels, of the loss of childhood protection and of the belief in parental omnipotence. They are living in a new phase of disillusionment – as Phillips (1994) puts it 'in the twilight of the Gods' – and yet they feel as if they lack any sense of effective power or influence over what is around them. They feel exposed, still helpless as children and unformed adults, and not at all sure of their capacity or value. Increasingly they are becoming more aware of their limitations and ultimately their mortality, and as yet unsure of what they can achieve.

Adolescents are, as such, in a peculiarly precarious and isolated position. They feel curiously disconnected from all that has held them together in the past, and confronted with all that is new and unfamiliar and potentially threatening in the future. They are unavoidably driven back into themselves and, for the time being, as they struggle to keep their balance and find a way forward, they take refuge as it were in the realm of narcissistic defence. It is always part of the eddy of adolescence that progressive and regressive trends swirl about with such unpredictable and varying force. Alongside the curiosity about what is new and the readiness for new dimensions of experience, there are the opposites and the yearning for the way it was before, where what is new or different could be felt as potentially destructive.

The grandiose and idealising solution

It is very much within this dynamic of regression – this narcissistic retreat to earlier modes and defensive patterns – that adolescents veer towards grandiose or idealising solutions (Kohut, 1972, 1977). Faced as they are with the vexing questions about self-coherence, value, potency, even existence, they resort unconsciously to the primitive defensive 'configurations' that Kohut has delineated so clearly. These underlie the adolescent experience and shape in one way or another what Greenberg has called 'the omnipotent quest during adolescence' (Greenberg, 1975).

Greenberg has captured how adolescents make use of what he calls 'magical manoeuvres' to deal with the underlying sense of narcissistic vulnerability and loss of omnipotence and to fill the 'aching void created by the dethronement of his objects'. He describes how adolescents invest in different kinds of surrogate objects which are idealised and experienced as carrying the very qualities that adolescents feel themselves to lack. The 'friend', the 'first heterosexual object choice', 'adults and older adolescents', the 'hero' and the peer group are all seen as restoring adolescents' sense of well-being – giving them a sense of narcissistic 'completion' and of effectiveness through identification and by proxy. Alternatively the self is invested with omnipotent power. 'The teenager temporarily takes himself as his love-object, investing himself with the omnipotence of the parents.' There is much, in other words, in adolescents' imagination and perception of themselves and the external world that is larger than life. Adolescents are in a sense full of themselves – self-preoccupied and innocently arrogant; they know it all, they are invincible and can ride alone. There is much too in their inclination that is counterphobic – taking risks, going to the brink, drawing close to the limits of their strengths and capacities. Equally, they are absorbed with strong infatuations and devotions to other people, known and not known, or to causes or activities that consume them and motivate them. Adolescents can identify with the purity and perfection of these others. It is out of these temporary self-creations that a real adult self can eventually be formed as adolescents gradually adjust and adapt to the demands of reality and their own realistic abilities.

Adolescence is thus a time of heightened narcissism, a necessary transitional period of realisation about the nature of the self, of its limitations and its relation to the outside world. Adolescence is inevitably difficult, bewildering, disconcerting, but equally it is energising, exciting and above all potentially very creative. The majority of adolescents make the most of it, feeling free to risk defeat and frustration, able to tolerate their imperfections and those of others, and ready to enjoy the excitements of the unknown. They can learn and have fun and they know (just about) when to stop – they can keep within the limits of their abilities. Most adolescents get by, some more robustly than others, depending on the core of well being and personal resource they have gained and built, largely from positive and affirmative parental love in childhood.

Vulnerable adolescents

There are many adolescents, however, who do not seem to have secure within themselves such a holding, inner core of strength and of self-belief. Various experiences in their lives have rendered them especially vulnerable in adolescence; more terrified than others of separation and independence; more fearful of the demands made on their minds both from within their bodies and from the outside world; and more exposed to feelings of inadequacy, insignificance and potential disintegration. Some may have experienced traumatic loss in early life as a result of parental death or separation; or overwhelming abuse either directly or indirectly, through living in situations of domestic violence. Others may have undergone complicated and confusing early parent–child relationships, set by the ambivalence and inconsistency of their parents which only served to exacerbate and make more frightening the process of separation in childhood. Others too may have been born with particular temperamental dispositions that have rendered them unusually susceptible to both traumatic and less extreme stresses of family life.

Adolescents with this kind of histories and sensibilities feel especially helpless and fearful of what will happen to them next. They lack confidence and feel betrayed and let down by those they have idealised and affronted by the reality of their own imperfections and limitations. The narcissistic defensive processes that are already characteristic of the adolescent state become in these more vulnerable adolescents more prominent. In their attempts to contend with their fears of passivity and loss of control, they are especially inclined to retreat into a pretend world of grandeur. Either they duck the frustrations and complexities of their actual experience by retaining a fantasy of their own omnipotence, or they revere idols who symbolically represent clarity and inviolability. They are inclined to withdraw from social interaction, fortifying themselves in grandiose or idealising fantasies which in turn serve to isolate them further from others. They build in effect an inner world of certainty and perfection which they struggle to protect at all costs against any incursion.

The effects of such narcissistic retreat can be seen in a wide range of adolescent disturbance. Adolescents who engage in reckless delinquent behaviour, for example, are often excessively taken up with an inflated image of themselves, at the cost of losing touch with the realistic consequences of their actions. Other adolescents may take refuge in various compulsive activities, such as drug or alcohol abuse, or computer game addictions, or eating disorders, which are extremely self-absorbing and often contain a great deal of omnipotent reverie. The lives of many of these adolescents are necessarily restricted, although they are able to function more of less adequately in the everyday course of life, attending school and work and having some sort of social life.

There are some adolescents, however, who remove themselves more extensively from the outside world (Wilson, 1988). Their withdrawal is not psychotic: their reality testing is intact and they have the capacity to relate appropriately to other people. It is rather that they have chosen to insulate themselves within an encapsulated inner world, immersed in private preoccupation and phantasy, and occupied in solitary activities. Their position is one of massive retrenchment, an extreme form of narcissistic retreat. Many drop out of school or work. They give up their studies and literally disappear into their rooms, often staying in bed throughout the day, only occasionally making limited forays out of the house. Their lives become set, stuck and very lonely. They effectively hole themselves up in self-created fortresses and quite actively, often violently fend off any threat of encroachment. Their self-imposed isolation of course is not absolute; it occurs in the proximity of others who are inevitably concerned. It functions both to defy and to torment those who are around – and paradoxically to call forth the very interference it seeks to resist.

Case illustration

Ronald, a 16-year-old boy was referred to me by a distraught mother who felt that she could no longer stand by watching her son 'do nothing'. He spent his time almost entirely at home: by day, watching television in the living room, and in the evening locking himself into his room. His mother thought that he read comics and played computer games. She knew that occasionally at night he went out – but she didn't know where he went. For the most part, Ronald made sure that he was not seen by the rest of his family. He completely ignored his father and became increasingly nasty and offensive to his mother and younger sister. The only sign of warmth or pleasure that he showed was in his relationship to his dog whom he fed and cared for tenderly.

Ronald's mother described him as a worrying child from the beginning. As a baby he cried and fretted a great deal. He was a restless toddler and slept poorly. He was especially clinging, attending nursery school and this worsened following the birth of his sister when he was aged 4 years. In infant school he started well enough and had a very close friendship with another boy who lived next door. This unfortunately came to a sudden end when the friend's family moved away. He was very upset by this and seemed to 'lose heart and give up' at school. In secondary school, he was frequently absent, leaving school in the middle of the morning and returning home. When he was 13, he was caught shoplifting with a group of other boys on a number of occasions and for a while hung around with them on the streets. Eventually he gave this up and for most of the time he was a loner. His one claim to fame was that he was a good cross-country runner and he ran for a local club in his fourth and fifth years. For a while he had a relationship with a girlfriend, but that soon seemed to drift away. Towards the end of his schooldays he was described as a sullen and withdrawn young man, rather awkward and gauche in his manner and just 'throwing away his chances'. He left school with poor GCSEs and did nothing for a year after leaving school.

There had apparently been no dramatic or disturbing events in his family history. The family had remained intact through his childhood with a supportive extended family nearby. Mother recalled how she had fallen ill when Ronald was 8 and that he and his sister had been cared for by her sister. His father at that time had been away on business. It was at that time that Ronald lost his close friend who moved out of the area.

I saw Ronald in once-weekly psychotherapy for 15 months. He initially complained about coming – 'I'm here on sufferance' – but in fact he did not miss a session during the entire length of the therapy. Ronald was a tall, rather plumpish young man, slightly sleepy and vague in his manner with a wrought and wary expression. Initially he was silent and resistant. He waited for my questions and then dismissed them. There was no point, he said, in coming; he had no problems, he had 'no feelings'. All that mattered was that he should be left alone. He knew why his mother had wanted him to see me, but he dismissed her concern – 'she's always making a fuss'. In the first few weeks, I chose not to press this issue, but instead looked for ways of finding some contact, however tenuous. Gradually, almost in spite of himself, he started to talk about his comics and his computer games. These were activities that clearly absorbed him and it soon became clear that he knew a great deal about both. His knowledge of the various heroes and villains in the comics was remarkably detailed and his understanding of computers seemed very impressive.

As the therapy became more established, so he became increasingly free and open in telling me more about all these interests. He was visibly very excited to have me as an audience. He boasted and bragged and looked for approval. For the most part he seemed to assume that I knew the characters that he was referring to and the technicalities as well as he did. He enjoyed quizzing me and catching me out and thereby demonstrating his superiority. Occasionally he became angry with my ineptitude and failure to pay attention to the many details he told me. I was inevitably left floundering.

There was much in all of this that was quite boyish, almost delightfully so in its innocence and excitement. And yet there was another side, something more pressured and desperate. When, for example, he described the activities of the various comic characters he became noticeably tense and harsh in his tone of voice. He clearly derived a great deal of sadistic pleasure from much of the violent behaviour that the comic heroes engaged in, and in his insistence on my going along with what he had to say there was also something ominously intimidating. These early sessions proceeded nevertheless remarkably smoothly, considering his initial almost obdurate resistance. It was clear, however, that the overall agenda of the sessions was very much set by him. In response to my interest and effort to make a connection with him, he filled the sessions with his own private preoccupations, to the exclusion of all else that might be of concern to his mother or the reasons for him being in therapy. He implicitly required me to follow and admire what he was doing and talking about. He sought in effect to have me under his control, within the orbit of his fascinations – rather than as someone separate, who might take another line of interest. There was in fact something quite sealed off about these early sessions, as if an 'external world' did not exist.

The spell, however, had to be broken. About 3 months after the start of therapy, I had two frantic telephone calls from Ronald's mother saying that things were getting worse. Ronald had in fact had a very violent row with his father and had locked himself in his room for the whole weekend. He had not come out to eat and was silent and his mother had been worried that he might have damaged himself. When I brought this information to Ronald in the next session his manner changed abruptly. He looked grey and tense and he avoided any eye contact with me. He fell silent again. Eventually, he asked 'What do you want to know?' I simply wondered what had been going through his mind since we last met. 'None of your business' was all he had to say. The session passed uncomfortably with nothing more to add. Similarly, several sessions proceeded in this way – 'I have nothing to say, I feel nothing'.

Gradually, however, in following sessions, he did begin to talk about what was on his mind – and not least about his family and other people. He hated his father and sister and he despised his mother – they were all 'stupid' and 'hypocrites'. His father was weak and untrustworthy. His sister was a 'pathetic girl' and his mother just 'snivelled and whined'. He had no time for any of them. As far as he was concerned they could 'suffer'. He was not prepared to explain this intensity of denigration and contempt, but from time to time he gave hints of how he had loathed his parents for the way they had rowed with each other and had nearly separated in the past. He remembered how his mother had been ill when he was a little boy; he conveyed not so much concern about her as of anger that she had left him in the care of his aunt.

The extent and power of his hatred for his family were alarming. He continued for several sessions in this vein to express yet more and more invective against them. This inevitably spread to other people outside the family for whom he said he had 'no regard' – middle-aged 'tarted up' women, children 'who pester', motorists who 'carve you up'. He condemned them all and vowed to have nothing more to do with anybody. And he added vehemently – 'if they mess with me, I'll kill 'em'.

After a month or so, this tirade subsided and he slowly returned to his interest in comics and computers – a world that he now called his 'comic zone'. It was as if he lived in two different worlds: a pleasurable world of his own making and under his own control; and a hostile world beyond his ken and altogether persecutory. His retreat seemed in many respects quite straightforward – simply away from the latter into the refuge of the former. As far as he was concerned, he needed no one and he had no intention of 'budging'. 'They can put up with it - sod 'em.' This same sentiment existed in the transference. Either I complied with his implicit demand that I take part in the comic zone on his terms, or I was to be dismissed.

The therapy now proceeded along a difficult tortuous path. There was a continuous tension between his requirement for me to remain within his 'comic zone', and my concern to keep alive the feelings that he had expressed and his difficulties in the outside world. To some extent, of course, I followed his preoccupations with his comic heroes, I listened to his stories, I remembered the characters and I took part in his quizzes. And, above all, I paid attention to the significance of these characters for him – their superpowers, their invincibility, their existence 'above us all'. But, especially against the background of mounting parental anxiety, he and I could not ignore his withdrawal and his avoidance of what was going on in his actual life. As time went on and the more I pressed, so his fury with his parents and so many others became more passionate. At the same time, he asserted ever more insistently his indifference for what happened and his own superiority. He had no need he said for education, for example, for he knew all there was to know about computers. He 'knew' too that he could always make a living 'writing comic books'. People simply did not know what he knew – and he had no intention of letting them know anyway.

The more he continued like this, the more he sought to dismiss and belittle me. He often mocked me and accused me of wanting to get him 'down and hoodwink' him – just like his father had done over the years. He was flippant and ridiculed me for being 'mad'. Periodically, however, something harder showed through, something more angry and menacing. This he just about managed to hold in check, although there were many times when he found my failure to remember all of the details of his 'comic zone' and my refusal to stop enquiring about his feelings and his activities outside the therapy room 'very annoying' – even as he put it 'deliberate and insulting'. He sustained his demand that I should 'shut up – and stop the smart talk' (i.e. my references to the difficulties that he had told me about in his life and his attempts not to have to 'think about them too much' because 'they're uncomfortable'). In spite of all of his protest and derision, however, he was able at times to listen and reflect,

albeit that he quickly got back to his 'comic zone'. He was never late for
sessions: he never totally stopped me from speaking and equally he
never tired of drawing my attention to 'what's in there?' (comic zone).

After about 7 months of therapy his mother telephoned again, this
time to tell me that, unless her son pulled himself together, she and her
husband were going to throw him out of the house. She reported that
there had been yet another violent row between Ronald and his father.
Ronald had also frightened his sister, threatening her with a knife. I, as
before, reported this telephone conversation to Ronald in the following
session. He was furious. 'She's got no right to be calling up.' ' She
doesn't care.' 'She's a bitch' and so forth. The more he ranted in this
way, the more he lost his composure – and the more he sought to dominate and daunt me: 'It's none of your business', 'keep your nose out of
it.' I dealt with this as before, acknowledging his anger and dissatisfac-
tion, and pointing out how desperately he tried to hide all this in his
'comic zone'. I also added, on this particular occasion, a question that I
had not put to him so simply before – 'What has hurt you so much in
the past to make you so angry now?' This took him by surprise. He was
silent for a moment and then spluttered 'Hurt, hurt; what do you mean,
bloody hurt!' Suddenly he was beside himself, his lips quivered, he was
close to tears. He got up from his chair and strode around the room
glaring down at me and raising his fist as if to hit me: 'Hurt! What hurt?
Who's hurt? I'm not hurt. I'll show you what hurt is.' For a few
moments he was incoherent. I did not move and I said no more and he
eventually sat back in his chair. In a cold and deliberate way he
informed me that I was stupid, that I understood nothing, that it was
always a waste of time to come and see me and, if I said anything more,
he would leave the room immediately. As far as he was concerned, nothing had got to him and what he did feel was his private business anyway.
It was a tense, frightening, quite distraught moment – but eventually I
was able to speak. I quietly said that I thought he had in fact felt hurt
and frightened a great deal – by his parents threatening to evict him –
and that in some way this had touched on other earlier experiences that
he had suffered in his life which had similarly made him feel useless and
unwanted and very angry. I said that I understood the appeal of the
comic zone – but he and I knew we could not ignore these feelings;
they mattered too much to him, and could not be ignored as they were
here in the therapy room.

He was quiet for a while and at one point left the room to go to the
toilet. When he returned he suddenly started to talk quite movingly
about the friend he had had at primary school who had moved away. He
remembered feeling very confused about it at the time – he just could
not understand why his friend had had to go. He had felt very let down
and hurt – and his mother being ill and his father being away had left
him feeling even more abandoned and confused than before. As he left

the session he apologised for yelling at me – he said he felt 'bad' about that and he hoped that I was not too upset.

Therapy continued for 8 months after that session. He returned for a while to the 'comic zone' and didn't give up his 'songs' of hatred about other people for a while. He held on to these, however, with less tenacity than before and, although always resistant, he did begin to think about 'changing my life'. He talked more about his childhood friend and, with greater candour than before, he recalled his lack of friends at school, the bullying he had been victim to and the overriding sense of betrayal that he felt in general. The idea of seeking revenge on all those who had let him down excited him still – and he could talk animatedly of the tales of vengeance that occurred in the comic stories. He was more amenable to my raising the destructive and self-destructive consequences of such revenge – and he at least could begin to reconsider whether or not his parents 'deserved it'. There was no prospect as far as he was concerned, however, of 'letting up' on his father, but he was opening up to the possibility of getting out of the home more – rather than 'digging himself' in all of his hatred.

In the last period of therapy, Ronald seemed to 'grow up'. He seemed more ready to leave his comic zone and develop his interest in computers further. He seemed less fraught and more able to laugh at himself – 'the loony in the attic' – and even to express some concern about his mother's health. He finally found himself a job in a computer firm which he could actually allow himself to say he enjoyed. He felt that 'therapy had worked', but, partly because of his new working hours and travel and partly because he felt 'he'd had enough for the time being', he decided to finish therapy.

Discussion

This boy preferred a world of his own. His immersion in his 'comic zone' insulated him from intolerable tensions in the external world and provided him with a wealth of possibility in phantasy that he felt was unattainable in reality. Growing up for him was not a pleasurable or exciting experience. He found it overwhelming and frightening – predominantly frustrating and humiliating. He was, as far as he could see, safer and stronger by himself.

Perhaps most disturbing – and most disruptive of his adolescence – was the hostility that he carried into his adolescence from his childhood. This was not necessarily manifest in his late childhood, but a growing sense of resentment seemed to characterise his early adolescence. His petty delinquency, truancy and under-achievement at school were indications that things were not right for him. His eventual isolation and evident rebuke of, and periodic attacks on, his parents were stronger, more trenchant expressions of discontent and anger. People in his family were made to suffer, to be left in the dark and feel uneasy. And people outside the family were avoided – for fear of what they might do (mess him about) and what he might do ('kill 'em').

His self-imposed exile (he banished himself from the outside world, and he banished others from his) seemed ever-increasingly complete, almost fortress like. He effectively snarled at all those outside whom he saw as traitors and persecutors; his contempt and denigration and exclusion of others gave vent to his hostility and equally preserved his illusion of his inviolability. He had, he felt, no need of others; he had no feelings, no desire or yearning that could be hurt or thwarted. His safety was himself – and his pleasure was within himself. In many ways, it was true that he truly loved himself. His comic characters gave solace and fortitude. They had all of the powers and attractions that he felt he lacked and that he could catch hold of through identification. These characters were unhurtable and invincible; they were also powerful – they could hurt and wreak havoc. Through their super-abilities, they could set things right – many of them triumphed over villains – and this had its own particular appeal to his own sense of injustice in his actual life.

This major narcissistic retrenchment served him well in many respects. Not only did it provide him with a place of safety, albeit illusory, but it also opened up a world in which he could feel good and enjoy a sense of control and strength. It was a plastic world in which he could elaborate fantasies of all sorts, not least of revenge and aggression. It could be said that in this elaboration, within the private confines of his room, he found an 'acceptable' way of expressing his violence. It was a form of self-containment. At the same time, it cocked a snook at those he wished to defy.

All of this suited him, both in his pathway through adolescence and in his own particular protest at his parents. His narcissistic retreat had both a developmental and an individual significance – it served to deal with adolescent anxieties in general and with the revived feelings of hurt and resentment that he brought forward from his childhood. The intensity of these feelings (and thus of the degree of narcissistic defensive response) is difficult to understand fully from the knowledge of the history given – but there are indications to suggest that he was from the beginning a sensitive 'difficult' infant, who may have encountered early obstacles to the attachment to his mother. He later endured levels of stress in his family and in the parental marriage which may in turn have been confusing and frightening and proved more than he could understand or cope with. His unusually close relationship to his schoolfriend may have been a sign of this stress and represented a pre-adolescent narcissistic defence against loss of faith in his parents – through devotion to an idealised friend. In these circumstances, the loss of his friend for reasons beyond his control may have constituted a major trauma in latency – which overlay earlier trauma.

This boy was a reluctant entrant to psychotherapy. There were many reasons, not least the many advantages accruing from his narcissistic defensive retreat, why he would not be motivated to change. He was in effect pushed into psychotherapy by his mother – and therapy therefore was something instantly to be resisted. The only possibility of any therapeutic movement could arise through his own recognition of the inadequacy of his narcissistic solution. Clearly, at some level, he was already aware of its limitations before he came to therapy – his life was restricted, he had few friends, he perceived the world as frightening. But through his denunciation of the outside world and his involvement in his inner world, he could hold off the reality, at least for the time being.

Psychotherapy had to proceed slowly in acknowledgement of this ambiguity – and for much of the beginning period of therapy it took place according to the dictates of this boy's narcissistic requirements. To have pressed 'reality' on him prematurely would have been to have risked his further retrenchment – either culminating in the termination of therapy on his part or leading to a form of false compliance. Time had to be taken to follow his lead and to relate to the world that he was so interested in. It was important to play – not only in the Winnicottian sense of establishing a necessary transitional area for personal exchange, but also in the spirit of adolescence – attending to both child-like and adult-like facets of his personality. The admixture of boyish delight and, as it were, manly severity was a striking feature of psychotherapy with this boy.

Within this broad setting, the psychotherapy took many forms – at times absorbed in the details and manoeuvrings of the various comic characters and the impressive facts of computer literacy, and at other times, struggling with the feelings and sensibilities that he had about himself and about his parents and others in his life. There were aspects of the transference that clearly reflected his defiance of his father and disappointment in his mother; he fought not to be taken over and he resisted any hint of dependency for fear of being let down. But what was most prominent as the therapy moved on was the development of more primitive narcissistic transferences. As he opened up his 'comic zone' so increasingly he sought to secure me within it as an admiring and devoted audience. His narcissistic need was to have me in attendance, following and affirming – and effectively mirroring benignly his achievements. Within this transference, I did not have the sense that I was other than what he wanted me to be – a part of his world – a 'self-object' (Kohut, 1972). His manner became quite imperious and arrogant, and the facets of himself that he so dreaded – his uselessness, his impotence, his stupidity – were conveniently projected on to me.

This was the mode that was set for much of the therapy, particularly in its middle phase. It was a way of proceeding that he effectively insisted upon in accordance with the demands of his narcissism. Psychotherapy could not have proceeded without passing through it – without some basis of his sense of affirmation and positive regard from me. Equally, it could not have progressed without his narcissistic retrenchment being challenged.

As much as he avoided or resisted, and with however much violence, he could not entirely evade the encroachments of the external world – the rebuff of his peers, the failure of his examination efforts and, of course, the criticism of his parents. No matter how much protection his narcissistic world offered, it could never be enough to withstand the pressure of the external world – and these pressures were inevitably experienced in therapy. Psychotherapy consisted of a constant tension between his narcissistic insularity and the demands of the outside world (much of which of course he internalised). The telephone calls from his mother into my office were part of these demands – they literally sounded the bell. Moments occurred in therapy that were unavoidably fraught and desperate and made the more poignant, the more I was perceived as no longer part of his narcissistic milieu, but different, separate and thereby threatening and betraying. These moments, although alarming ,were not in fact destructive – in the context of the whole therapy – but were on the contrary productive of change. What was striking in the midst of these moments and in their aftermath.was his increased acknowledgement of his vulnerability, of his 'hurt' feelings and of his fears – and most notably of the loss of his childhood friend who stood for so much in his early life to do with loyalty and attachment. The therapy was able to move on on the basis of the insights of these moments towards greater integration and an acknowledgement of the demands of reality. Clearly by the end of therapy, this process had not been completed – but enough had been achieved to facilitate this adolescent to join up in the mainstream of life. He of course did not relinquish all of his phantasies and preoccupations – but effectively they interfered less with his ordinary adaptation to ordinary life and the development of his abilities in relation to other people. He himself thought 'therapy had worked'.

References

Blos P (1962). *On Adolescence: A Psychoanalytic Interpretation.* New York: Free Press.

Greenberg H (1975). The widening gyre: transformations of the omnipotent quest during adolescence. *International Review of Psycho-Analysis* 2: 231.

Kohut H (1972). Thoughts on narcissism and narcissistic rage. *Psychoanalytic Study of the Child* 27: 360–400.

Kohut H (1977). *The Restoration of the Self.* New York: International Universities Press.

Phillips A (1994). *On Flirtation.* London: Faber.

Wilson P (1988). The impact of cultural changes on the internal experience of the adolescent. *Journal of Adolescence* 11: 271–86.

Chapter 6
Between narcissistic and more mature object relating: narcissism and the couple

STANLEY RUSZCZYNSKI

In 'Analysis terminable and interminable', considered by some to be his clinical legacy, Freud writes about both the potential and the limitations of psychoanalysis as a therapeutic method. This realism extends to his view of human nature. He writes, 'A normal ego . . . is, like normality in general, an ideal fiction. The abnormal ego . . . is unfortunately no fiction. Every normal person, in fact, is only normal on the average. His ego approximates to that of the psychotic in some part or other and to a greater or lesser extent' (Freud, 1937, p. 235). In this chapter I explore this appraisal of the 'normal person' by examining the nature of the individual's object relations, with particular reference to love relationships.

Individuals and relationships

There will inevitably be times, in all intimate couple relationships, when one or both partners, consciously and unconsciously, are more preoccupied with themselves than with the other or their relationship. The capacity to tolerate this inevitable tension between the appropriate and necessary separateness of each of the individuals and the requirements of their mutually aspired-to partnership is a significant sign of the health of any relationship. However, this same dynamic tension between individual needs and the needs of the partnership also provides the structure that invites the unconscious enactment of less mature and more primitively organised ways of relating. In such less mature interaction, the separateness of the self and the other is not recognised, respected and valued but is denied, or there is a seeking to control or attack the other whose difference and separateness is felt to be persecutory; also the other is not related to in their fullness but more in relation to particular aspects which come to be experienced as dominant. (See Ruszczyn-ski (1995) where these ideas are also explored.)

Such a lack of capacity to move with concern from individual needs to those of the partner and of their relationship, will be demonstrated either by an inability to establish or sustain a meaningful intimate rela-tionship or by producing a highly fused undifferentiated relationship.

Psychoanalytic psychotherapy with couple relationships offers a rich opportunity to explore the nature of the individual's ways of relating both intrapsychically and interpersonally. The clinical question that emerges is whether there is the potential for movement between what we may refer to as narcissistic to more mature object relating. Such a statement, however, requires a definition of what is meant by both narcissism and mature object relating. Contemporarily we might in fact be most interested in exploring *the relationship between these two states of mind*, which Bion, for example, echoing Freud, refers to as the differentiation between the psychotic and non-psychotic parts of the personality (Bion, 1957).

The intimate couple may be said to come together and construct the nature of their interaction substantially on the basis of a mutual uncon-scious acceptance of each other's projections which creates a sense of recognition and attachment. The unconscious drive is for *defensive purposes*, disowning parts of the self and locating them in the other who is obliged to carry the projected attributes, and also for *developmental purposes*, where the other's capacity to contain and metabolise the projected attributes may enable the projector to take them back in a form now considered to be more acceptable and manageable. In this way the intimate couple relationship may be considered to be a mutual enactment of intrapsychic conflicts and object relations in the daily living of the interpersonal relationship (Ruszczynski, 1992).

Psychoanalysis, therefore, with its focus on intrapsychic conflict, offers a particularly useful theoretical understanding of the intimate couple relationship and clinical practice with couples (Dicks, 1967; Ruszczynski, 1993). It is perhaps surprising that, with a very few excep-tions, especially in Britain, psychoanalysts have not taken more interest in the marital relationship as a focus of clinical and theoretical research (see Scharff, 1993). After all, Freud, while paying no particular attention in his writings to marital and family life, noted that transference – a concept central to psychoanalytic theory and practice – arises sponta-neously in all human relationships (see Balint, 1968). Klein, in her writ-ings, agrees. She writes: 'In some form or other transference operates throughout life and influences all human relationships' (Klein, 1952, p. 48). The love relationship may be said to be a form of transference rela-tionship, with internal object relations substantially shaping the nature of the couple's interaction with each other.

Anaclitic or narcissistic relationships

In 1914 Freud suggested that the study of the erotic life of human beings shows two types of intimate relations: that which he calls an anaclitic (or attachment) type of love, fundamentally a love of the object which has nourished or protected; and that which he calls a narcissistic type of love, a love of what the person himself is, was or would like to be, which Freud understood to be an objectless state.

Freud writes:

> We have, however, not concluded that human beings are divided into two sharply differentiated groups, according as their object-choice conforms to the anaclitic or to the narcissistic type; we assume that both kinds of object-choice are open to each individual, though he may show a preference for one or the other. We say that a human being has originally two sexual objects – himself and the woman who nurses him - and in doing so we are postulating a primary narcissism in everyone, which in some cases manifests itself in a dominating fashion in his object choice
>
> *Freud (1914, p. 88)*

As a result of her clinical work with children, Klein postulated very early child–mother relating. In an unintegrated way, from the very beginning the infant experiences a satisfying good object and a separate frustrating bad object. The impulses felt towards the mother are projected into her and contribute to colouring the nature of the object subsequently introjected. This normal process of projection and introjection builds up, within the infant, an inner world made up of a variety of relationships to different objects or, rather more accurately, part-objects. As Klein puts it:

> Every external experience is interwoven with . . . phantasies and on the other hand every phantasy contains elements of actual experience.
>
> *Klein (1952, p. 54)*

It is not, therefore, as Freud wrote, that there is an initial objectless stage of development. On the contrary, primitive relating is a relating to aspects of the self and to aspects of the other and, because of the fragmented nature of earliest experience, such relating may be overwhelming in its emotional force.

Klein's concept of projective identification (Klein, 1946, 1955) refers to an unconscious phantasy of splitting off and projecting impulses and aspects of the self into an object which then becomes identified as possessing those attributes projected into it. This process may be used in phantasy to dominate and control the object, as a way of keeping the projection intact in the other, or as a way of avoiding the awareness of separateness and difference and all the anxieties that this awareness might produce.

Schizoid mechanisms

In the course of the formulation of her ideas about psychic development, Klein introduced the concepts of the paranoid–schizoid and depressive positions, understood to be fluid constellations of anxieties, defences and types of object relations. The most important difference between the two positions is in relation to the degree of increasing psychological integration as the depressive position is approached, leading to a sense of wholeness in the self and a capacity for concern for the other. Although the paranoid–schizoid position predates the depressive position and is more primitive in its form, a continuous dynamic movement takes place between the two so that neither position and its anxieties, defences and types of object relating dominate with any degree of permanence (Steiner, 1992). The development of this understanding of the schizoid processes of splitting, projection, and introjective and projective identification, operating from the start of life, suggests a particular understanding of narcissism and narcissistic object relations.

Klein herself only ever made two direct references to narcissism (Klein, 1946, 1952), although when she did so it was in a way that remains very familiar to our understanding today. She writes:

> [A] typical feature of schizoid object-relations is their narcissistic nature which derives from the infantile introjective and projective processes. For . . . when the ego-ideal is projected into another person, this person becomes predominantly loved and admired because he contains the good part of the self. Similarly, the relation to another person on the basis of projecting bad parts of the self into him is of a narcissistic nature, because in this case as well the object strongly represents one part of the self . . . When these parts have been projected excessively into another person, they can only be controlled by controlling the other person.
>
> *Klein (1946, p. 13)*

With the paranoid–schizoid position consisting of a preponderance of processes of splitting, projection and introjection, this position may be considered to be synonymous with narcissistic object-relations. As Steiner puts it:

> One of the consequences of projective identification is that the subject relates to the object not as a separate person with his own characteristics but as if relating to himself. He may ignore aspects of the object which do not fit the projection or he may control and force or persuade the object to enact the role required of him.
>
> *Steiner (1993, p. 42)*

The concept of projective identification therefore helps us substantially to understand the individual who, as Freud put it, loves (according to the narcissistic type of love) 'what he himself is, was or would like to be' (Freud, 1914). We can now see that such a love of the other is based on the fact that, in phantasy, parts of the self and internal objects have been projected into the other who is then identified as possessing these attributes and it is this that makes this other so attractive to the narcissistic individual (Joseph, 1989). The concept of projective identification may also enable us to differentiate between a narcissistic state, which involves a withdrawal to an idealised or denigrated internal object, and a more established, long-term psychic structure which organises object relations in a particular way.

Any new life situation or stage of development may arouse fundamental anxieties relating to insecurity and lack of control over the internal and external environment. Such anxieties may, therefore, arouse the defences and types of object relations of the paranoid–schizoid position. Such object relations, although in a healthy relationship only temporary and eventually worked through to the depressive position, are not fundamentally different from those experienced by couples and individuals who more continually relate in this way. This movement between the paranoid–schizoid and depressive positions may be considered to be synonymous with the movement between more narcissistic and more mature forms of object relating.

Steiner has recently stressed the complexity, rigidity and highly organised nature of the defensive processes employed by those individuals whose internal world is *consistently* organised by more primitive and pathological splitting and projective processes. He coins the evocative term 'psychic retreat' (Steiner, 1993) to delineate this particular psychic organisation, the fixedness of which significantly differentiates it from more temporary state of paranoid–schizoid/narcissistic withdrawal.

So, in this way, we can differentiate between a temporary, defensive narcissistic withdrawal, which may represent a part of the constant movement between the paranoid–schizoid and the depressive positions, and the more rigidly organised narcissistic psychic organisation, which constructs a more inflexible structure locking the individual and/or the intimate couple into pathological object relations.

The interesting clinical question in relation to the couple is whether the committed couple relationship *institutionalises* the pathological psychic structure, or whether the more healthy part of the couple, even when the relationship is primarily under the dominance of paranoid–schizoid anxieties, defences and object relations, allows for *some* psychic work to take place *in the relationship* which neither individual could manage alone.

There is no doubt that sometimes a couple relationship does atrophy psychically into a rigid pattern of interaction, and may on occasion produce something that may be described as a projective gridlock (Morgan, 1995) or a claustrum type of relationship (Fisher, 1994), within which there is really no opportunity for the fluidity of movement between the more primitive and the more mature ways of relating. If both members of the couple are substantially under the sway of the more narcissistic/paranoid–schizoid type of object relating, a rigidified *folie à deux* may be established which might be extremely resistant or even immune to psychotherapeutic intervention. However, it may also be possible to consider that the couple relationship contains some residue of the more healthy and developmental aspects inherent in all relationships – even if this is only in one partner – which may be drawn on to contain and process the enactments of the more primitive object relations. In the same way that Freud refers to the normal and abnormal ego, and Bion refers to the psychotic and non-psychotic parts of the personality, we may, in parallel, refer to a differentiation between the more defensive and the more developmental aspects of marital relationships (Ruszczynski, 1992).

In this context, the role of the psychoanalytic marital psychotherapist may be crucial in offering the couple, in the working through of the transferences that will emerge in the psychotherapeutic situation, the containment (in Bion's terms) through which they can secure or re-establish the containment inherent in a good-enough intimate relationship. Initially, the psychotherapist is likely to be induced into the projective network of the couple's interaction, to the point, as in individual psychoanalytic work, of transference–countertransference enactments (Sandler, 1976; Brenman Pick, 1985; Joseph, 1989). If, however, again as in work with individuals, the psychotherapist can process and detoxify the experience that he or she has been enticed into, and subsequently offer understanding and insight into the functioning of the projective system operated by the couple, they may be able to mediate the rigidity and inflexibility of their interaction and take a step towards establishing the containment inherent in their relationship. Without being seduced by therapeutic enthusiasm, we may be sustained in our clinical experiences by recalling Joseph's considered view that, providing, of course, we can tune into it, 'projective identification is by its very nature a kind of communication, *even in cases where this is not its aim or its intention*' (Joseph, 1989, p. 170, my emphasis). Working in the cauldron of the intimate couple relationship, it may sometimes be extremely difficult not to become overwhelmed and trapped in the projective system. It is for this reason that some couples are better worked with clinically by two therapists working together with the couple in a foursome (Lyons, 1973; Ruszczynski, 1993a).

Destructive narcissism

Steiner's work on the psychic retreat, as referred to earlier, is based substantially on that of Rosenfeld who refined the understanding of narcissistic object-relations in an important way when he emphasised the notion of 'destructive narcissism' (Rosenfeld, 1971). This was already briefly referred to in Klein's writings (for example, see quote from Klein (1946) above), and Rosenfeld's researches further showed how the narcissistic state is not necessarily a withdrawal to, or an identification with, a good internalised object but may be a withdrawal to a more destructive internal object. This then acts as an internal 'Mafia' or 'saboteur' to defeat the efforts of the more benign relating part of the self. Destructive narcissism is understood to be the product of the more envious aspects of the self: the more omnipotent self-sufficient part of the self is identified with and attacks the more dependent part of the self which may wish to form attachments and hence arouse the destructive envy of the narcissistic self.

A contribution from Balint

In passing, it is interesting to note that Michael Balint, within his own theoretical framework, also rejected the idea of a stage of development before object relating. He refers to primitive forms of object relating in which 'the object is taken for granted' (Balint, 1968, p. 70). This may be seen as comparable to the phantasy of the domination and control of the object explicitly understood to be a central aspect of Klein's concept of projective identification.

Balint's description of this primitive type of object relating is very evocative of the pathological and destructive ways in which some more disturbed couples relate to each other. He writes:

> A common feature of all these primitive forms of object relationship is that in it the object is taken for granted; the idea that an indifferent object exists and that it should be changed into a cooperative partner by 'the work of conquest' has not yet arisen . . . only one partner may have wishes, interests and demands of his own; without any further need for testing, it is taken for granted that the other partner, the object . . . will automatically have the same wishes, interests and expectations . . . If any hitch or disharmony between subject and object occurs, the reaction to it will consist of loud and vehement symptoms suggesting processes either of a highly aggressive and destructive, or profoundly disintegrative, nature, i.e. either as if the whole world, including the self, would have been smashed up, or as if the subject would have been flooded with pure and unmitigated aggressive–destructive impulses.
>
> *Balint (1968, p. 70)*

This 'hitch' or 'disharmony' between the subject and the object may be understood to be the subject's realisation of both dependence on the object and the object's separateness. In the paranoid–schizoid/narcissistic position, such awareness may lead to the arousal of destructive envy, splitting to the point of disintegration and hatred.

Narcissism and envy

Segal writes that:

> The discovery of the object gives rise to hate. One could describe envy in a very similar way. The way primary envy is described by Melanie Klein is as a spoiling hostility at the realisation that the source of life and goodness lies outside . . . [E]nvy and narcissism are like two sides of a coin. Narcissism defends us against envy . . . (and) . . . if, with Melanie Klein, one contends that awareness of an object relation and, therefore, envy exists from the beginning, narcissism could be seen as a defence against envy and therefore to be more related to the operation of the death instinct and envy than to libidinal forcers.
>
> *Segal (1983, pp. 270–1)*

Such an understanding of narcissism stresses how destructive it is of real object relating.

In Paula Heimann's description of primitive object relations she writes that:

> The essential difference between infantile and mature object relations is that, whereas the adult conceives of the object as existing independently of himself, for the infant *it always refers in some way to himself*. It exists only by value of its function for the infant.
>
> *Heimann (1952, p. 142, my emphasis)*

Such self-reference informs much of the object relating of the narcissistic individual and is perhaps close to the more colloquial understanding of narcissism. Unless the object always complies with this domination by the subject, there are very likely to be times when the subject fails in securing the required self-reference. This may result in a volatile swing between the idealisation of the compliant object and the denigration of the independent object. With such a tendency towards volatility, more narcissistically structured relationships are likely to be very unstable and unpredictable.

Clinical illustration

I will now give some clinical material from psychoanalytic work with a couple to illustrate some of the concepts I have been discussing.

I have been seeing Mr and Mrs A, twice a week, for about 18 months. They sought psychotherapeutic help because of their concern about growing tension and distress between them which, at times, exploded into serious and bitter arguments, occasionally including physical exchanges. The couple were in their late thirties, had been together for about 8 years and had a toddler. They were in the same profession, worked in sister institutions and were both actively pursuing their professional ambitions.

On one particular occasion, as the first session of the week got under way, I noticed that Mr A looked very tense and agitated and was regularly turning to his wife and looking at her in an openly aggressive way. Mrs A spoke first and said that a couple of days earlier Mr A had been made a very exciting job offer which could substantially enhance his professional ambitions and therefore needed serious consideration. Ever since then, she said, the two of them had been in a state of high tension and antagonism and were fighting. She added that she felt attacked by her husband and was very confused, distressed and angry.

Almost immediately the couple engaged in their argument and I soon observed that, as Mrs A attempted to offer her thoughts, views and encouragement about the prospective job – as invited to do so by her husband – Mr A kept angrily insisting that his wife was totally disinterested and simultaneously accused her of trying to dictate to him how he should proceed. This oscillating perception of his wife was quite extraordinary and almost bizarre. Eventually, repeatedly wrong-footed, Mrs A was left in a state of spluttering confusion, driven to impotent speechlessness by her husband's attacks on her.

I found myself unsure whether to trust my own observations and experience, and was also left feeling confused, anxious that I was not understanding the situation and feeling somewhat impotent. I felt isolated from the couple and their experience, just as they were from each other.

I then noticed that Mr A now looked less tense and seemed to be calmer. He turned to me and in a considered way explained, perhaps with a slightly patronising tone, that he was in the final stages of setting up a number of projects for himself which, taken together, made up a very viable and interesting work plan. He was not sure exactly how this compared with the new job offer but, he said very calmly, he was probably going to pursue his own scheme.

I was struck by the dramatic contrast between Mr A's mood and manner now and how he had been earlier in the session, and also how his thoughtful state of mind compared with how I observed his wife to be. I was also aware of my own anxious discomfort in relation to the session so far. It seemed as if both Mrs A and I in the countertransference, had been rendered confused, anxious and speechless whereas Mr A appeared to be thoughtful and clear.

I came to wonder whether this rather dramatic change in Mr A and the apparent difference now between his state of mind and that of both his wife and mine, suggested that splitting and projective identification had taken place between us. The uncertainty and conflict that the enticing job offer would probably have created was completely absent from Mr A. His wife, however, as I observed her, and I, in my countertransference, were feeling confused and unsure and rendered somewhat impotent.

I began to wonder whether the job offer had disturbed Mr A's equilibrium. Rather than being seen as something tempting, for which he could
feel ambivalence and uncertainty, or excitement and gratitude, the job
offer may have been experienced as a challenge to the self-constructed
work plans that Mr A had made for himself. The conflict and uncertainty
about how he should proceed could have felt like an attack on his sense
of self by a persecutory bad-object. Further, the very fact that it was such
a tempting offer could have provoked his feelings of envy: someone else
had something to give that he wanted. Finally, if he were to accept the
job offered he would be working under the authority of his new
employer rather than be in charge of his own planned projects. This
could raise anxieties about dependence and of not being in control.

Rather than emotionally engage in these various conflicts and anxieties, Mr A split off his feelings of uncertainty, confusion, and fear of loss
of power and control, projected them into his objects whom he then
identified as feeling the conflicts and confusion, and left himself identified with a calm and certain self again. This identification with an internal good-object could be understood as a narcissistic withdrawal,
created by processes of splitting and projective identification primarily
with his wife, and possibly with me. Mr A was relating to Mrs A as if she
were confused about whether he should take up the job or not. In this
way he was relating to what he had projected into her (i.e. his own
confusion and conflict) rather than to what she herself was trying to say
to him. This would, therefore, produce a narcissistic object relationship,
constructed substantially by the splitting and projective processes,
rather than a more mature object relationship in which the other's individuality and separateness are recognised and related to with some
interest and concern.

A similar dynamic is experienced in Mr A's relationship with me in the
transference. Can I be allowed to be the employer/psychotherapist who
offers potentially interesting psychotherapeutic work or does he turn
down my offered interpretations and continue to use his old familiar
defences and ways of relating? Does he put himself in a position of
dependency on the psychotherapy and me or does he retain his narcissistic self-reliance, identifying himself with a near-idealised internal
object constructed partly by identifying with and introjecting my capacities for thought and reflection, leaving me in the countertransference
feeling uncertainty and confusion?

Mr A's interaction with his wife can be understood in a similar way to
this – she too has the potential to be turned to as an object who may
have something to offer him and in this way arouse envy and unconscious attacks.

However, Mrs A also had a part to play in the interaction between
them, and in the creation of Mr A's state of mind. It emerged that she
herself had been disturbed by the job offer made to her husband

because, in fact, it had aroused her envy, which she very quickly split off and denied to herself. This left her feeling confused and ambivalent about her support for her husband and persecuted by guilt. Unconsciously, she had attempted to disown this reaction in herself and to project it into her husband. She could then identify herself with a good internal object wishing to be helpful to her husband. However, this evacuative projective process, including the split off and projected envy, was unconsciously experienced by Mr A as an attack. He then found himself dealing with a Mrs A who was consciously supporting him and, simultaneously, projecting into him in an aggressive way in her attempt to deal with her envy, confusion and guilt. This latter meshed in with Mr A's own envy and confusion and so aroused his paranoid anxieties against which he defended himself by violent splitting and projection.

It was this complex set of splitting and evacuative projective identification which created the fights between them, both at home and in the consulting room. Each became easily dominated by the more paranoid anxieties that call up the more primitive or destructive narcissistic defences and types of object relations.

In this brief illustration I have tried to show how the anxieties and defensive processes of the paranoid–schizoid position are brought into play by feelings of envy and dependence. Splitting and projective identification are then employed to manage these anxieties in an attempt to re-establish some sense of psychic equilibrium. Persecutory experiences are dealt with by projective identification which obliges the other to carry the disturbing attributes leaving the projector free to identify with a more benign sense of self.

In a couple relationship the partner often becomes the object for the projective mechanisms but it is likely that both partners will have some emotional reaction to the issue in hand. This may then produce a highly complex web of anxieties and splitting and projective identification as defences against these persecutory feelings. In this more primitive interaction, narcissistic withdrawal to an internal good-object or part of the self becomes the predominant form of the self's expression, with an attempt made for the other to carry the disowned attributes. Such a preponderance of splitting and projective identification produces a volatile relationship with little capacity for reflection or genuine concern for the other.

It could be argued that the enactment of these narcissistic object relations in the interpersonal dynamic between the couple externalises the pathological personality organisation. If one partner in the couple is less under the influence of the more paranoid–schizoid anxieties and defences, his or her capacity for thought and concern for the other may present the potential for a more containing experience within the couple relationship. However, at the same time, the more destructive aspects of the paranoid–schizoid position will attack this in the partner and so undermine the containing potential in the intimate relationship. This sabotaging may unconsciously be recognised by one or both partners and lead them to seek psychotherapeutic help and then, of course, the psychotherapy becomes the target for the attack as it is seen to be in opposition to the existing more primitive ways of relating.

Summary

The tension within the self between the more narcissistic and more mature object relations is understood to be present in all individuals. In this way, Freud's view of the universal nature of what he calls 'normal' and 'abnormal' ego within each individual is supported. This is understood to be a description of all individuals given that there is potential for constant movement between the more primitive anxieties and defences of the paranoid–schizoid position and the more mature capacity for ambivalence and concern for the other of the depressive position. *All* individuals are, at times, likely to experience the more primitive anxieties and respond more narcissistically. Some individuals are more regularly under the influence of such anxieties and defences, and the more disturbed can be understood as consistently living in this state of mind and object relating.

In this chapter I have suggested that this oscillation will be aroused and enacted in the intimate couple relationship. As a result of its potential for intimacy and longevity, a couple relationship potentially has both the capacity to institutionalise pathologically such object relating, via a projective gridlock (Morgan, 1995), into an anti-developmental psychic retreat (Steiner, 1993) and the potential, made available by the possible containment inherent in the more healthy aspects of the couple relationship, to manage, process and contain the movements between narcissistic and more mature object relating.

References

Balint E (1968). Unconscious communications between husband and wife. In: WG Joffe (Ed.), *What is Psychoanalysis?* Institute of Psychoanalysis/Ballière Tindall & Cassell. Republished in S Ruszczynski (Ed.), *Psychotherapy With Couples*. London: Karnac Books, 1993.

Balint M (1968). *The Basic Fault*. London: Tavistock Publications.

Bion WR (1957). Differentiation of the psychotic from the non-psychotic parts of the personality. *International Journal of Psycho-Analysis* 38: 266–76. (Reprinted in *Second Thoughts*, pp. 43–64 (1984). London: Karnac Books.)

Brenman Pick I (1985). Working through in the counter-transference. *International Journal of Psycho-Analysis* 66: 157–66.

Dicks H (1967). *Marital Tensions*. London: Routledge & Keegan Paul.

Fisher J (1994). Intrusive identification, the claustrum and the couple. *Journal of the British Association of Psychotherapists* 24: Summer.

Freud S (1914). On narcissism: An introduction. *The Complete Psychological Works of Sigmund Freud*, standard edition, vol. 14. London: Hogarth Press.

Freud S (1937). Analysis terminable and interminable. *The Complete Psychological Works of Sigmund Freud*, standard edition, vol. 23. London: Hogarth Press.

Heimann P (1952). Certain functions of projection and introjection in early infancy. In: M Klein, P Heimann, S Issacs, J Riviere (Eds), *Developments in Psycho-Analysis*. London: Hogarth Press.

Joseph B (1989). *Psychic Equilibrium and Psychic Change*. London: Routledge.

Klein M (1946). Notes on some schizoid mechanisms. *International Journal of Psycho-Analysis* 27: 99–110. (Reprinted in *The Writings of Melanie Klein*, pp. 1–24 (1975). Vol. 3. London: Hogarth Press.)

Klein M (1952). The origins of transference. *International Journal of Psycho-Analysis* 33: 433–8. (Reprinted in *The Writings of Melanie Klein*, pp. 48–56 (1975). Vol. 3. London: Hogarth Press.)

Klein M (1955). On identification. In: M Klein, P Heimann, R Money-Kyrle (Eds), *New Directions in Psycho-analysis*. London:Karnac Books, 1977.

Lyons A (1973). Therapeutic interventions in relation to the institution of marriage. In: R Gosling (Ed.), *Support, Innovation and Autonomy*. Tavistock Clinic Golden Jubilee Papers. London: Tavistock Publications. (Reprinted in S Ruszczynski (Ed.), *Psychotherapy with Couples* (1993). London: Karnac Books.)

Morgan M (1995). The projective gridlock: a particular form of projective identification in couple relationships. In: S Ruszczynski, J Fisher (Eds), *Intrusiveness and Intimacy in the Couple*. London: Karnac Books.

Rosenfeld HA (1971). A clinical approach to the psychoanalytic theory of the life and death instinct: an investigation into the aggressive aspects of narcissism. *International Journal of Psycho-Analysis* 52: 169–78.

Ruszczynski S (1992). Some notes towards a psychoanalytic understanding of the couple relationship. *Psychoanalytic Psychotherapy* 6: 33–48.

Ruszczynski S (Ed.) (1993). *Psychotherapy With Couples*. London: Karnac Books.

Ruszczynski S (1993a). Thinking about and working with couples. In S Ruszczynski (Ed.), *Psychotherapy with Couples*. London: Karnac Books.

Ruszczynski S (1995). Narcissistic object relating. In S Ruszczynski, J Fisher (Eds), *Intrusiveness and Intimacy in the Couple*. London: Karnac Books.

Sandler J (1976). Countertransference and role-responsiveness. *International Review of Psycho-Analysis* 3: 43–7.

Scharff D (1993). Foreword. In: S Ruszczynski (Ed.), *Psychotherapy with Couples*. London: Karnac Books.

Segal H (1983). Some clinical implications of Melanie Klein's work: emergence from narcissism. *International Journal of Psycho-Analysis* 64: 269–76.

Steiner J (1992). The equilibrium between the paranoid–schizoid and the depressive positions. In R Anderson (Ed.), *Clinical Lectures on Klein and Bion*. London: Routledge.

Steiner J (1993). *Psychic Retreats*. London: Routledge.

Chapter 7
Narcissistic displacement in childbearing

JOAN RAPHAEL-LEFF

> Parental love which is so moving and at bottom so childish is nothing but the parents' narcissism born again . . .
>
> *Freud (1914, p. 91)*

I shall use this quotation as a springboard to explore the dual nature of early parent–child interaction – both the narcissistic use the adult makes of the child and effects on the child's own narcissism of internalisation of this identificatory relationship. I locate my exploration in the arena of childbearing – the moment when the grown-up child has to confront becoming a parent in his or her own right.

It is almost 100 years since the term 'narcismus' was first used by Nacke (1899, cited by Freud, 1914) to denote one's own body treated as a sexual object, and 80 years since Freud extended the term to include relationships in his treatise 'On narcissism', (Freud, 1914) (a strange paper, which he says (p. 70) 'had a difficult labour and bears all the marks of a corresponding deformation'). He depicts adult narcissistic love as a disturbance in libidinal development leading to seeking oneself as a love-object.

Since then the concept has undergone many vicissitudes, both as an indication of pathology and as a feature of normal development. Latter-day psychoanalytic literature abounds with theories about structuring of the *child's* healthy narcissism and emergent sense of self through the medium of empathic mirroring (Winnicott, 1967; Kohut, 1977). Conversely, pathological narcissism is attributed to caregiver unresponsiveness resulting in the child's ego depletion caused by varying degrees of collusion ('false self' – Winnicott, 1967) or arrested development (horizontal or vertical splitting between an archaic grandiose self and idealised object – Kohut, 1977). Another school (positing what Symington (1993) calls 'phobia' as opposed to 'trauma' theories) stresses not environmental deficits but the effect of the infant's own omnipotent phantasies (Freud, 1914) and envious/aggressive projection of parts of the self onto the relational exchange (Klein, 1946) and grandiose denial of dependency on a projectively idealised object (Kernberg, 1984). A third position stresses the mixture of both intrapsychic and interpersonal factors – defensive internalisation of the tantalising emotionally unavailable caregiver (Fairbairn, 1952), pathogenic caregiving causing failure to progress from dyadic to triadic relations (Mollon, 1993), or intentional turning away from the source of emotional life, the internalised 'lifegiver' (Symington, 1993).

I do not wish to enter here into discussion of the thorny issues of primary versus secondary narcissism, ego-ideal versus idealised object-love, nor yet of positive and/or negative narcissism. In this chapter my focus will be on the relatively ignored area of *perinatal phantasies* – restructuring of a *parent's* narcissism through positive or negative representations of procreation, gestation and parenthood, and the effect on the baby of internalising unconscious parental representations. To make this point, I draw on my work with several hundred people on the verge of childbearing – some undergoing fertility treatment, others expectant parents or new mothers, fathers and babies seen individually, in pairs or groups preconceptually, throughout pregnancy and/or the first postnatal years in a clinical practice devoted to issues based around reproductivity (one to five times per week psychoanalysis or therapy for 2–12 years). Yet others, seen in a research context, were interviewed in depth at various points before and after the birth.

As I have elaborated elsewhere (Raphael-Leff, 1993, 1995), most would-be parents hold a variety of representations of their awaited baby and personal ideas about ideal parenting which, following a birth, tend to abate gradually as phantasy babies are relinquished with increasing recognition of the neonate as an individual, and reality as flawed. However, when 'fixed' phantasies and narcissistic imagery predominate, unless mitigated by therapy during the pregnancy or early parenthood, after the birth the imagined scenario continues to overshadow the real one, thereby affecting parent–child interaction (Raphael-Leff, 1991).

Narcissism revitalised

A pertinent question at this point is why parental narcissism and concomitant phantasies flourish around childbearing? In my clinical experience, there are several contributing factors.

First, *childbearing promises perpetuity*. As Freud pointed out, 'in the unconscious every one of us is convinced of his own immortality' (Freud, 1915, p. 289). The desire/decision to have a child serves to reinforce our narcissistic disavowal of death. Childbearing offers a means of bridging the 'twofold function' of an individual – as a unique person in his or her own right and as a mere 'mortal vehicle of an immortal substance' as Freud called us. On a reproductive level, even germ-cells '. . . behave in a completely narcissistic fashion' (Freud, 1920, p. 50) coalescing to express self-interest in guaranteeing the 'immortality of the living substance' (p. 56). As Badcock (1994) points out, such narcissism reflects 'the value of the organism to its genes' (p. 110). In parallel, we may say that childbearing reinforces grandiose god-like aspirations of self-perpetuation.

Second, in any transitional period, *uncertainty breeds speculative expectations*. These usually manifest as a proliferation of phantasies, daydreams, superstitious or magical thinking, and introspective ruminations which serve the dual desires of exploring the unknown and having omnipotent narcissistic control over it. Pregnancy (and particularly gestation of a first child) is a time of vulnerable liminality: a subjective domain hanging betwixt and between past and future; self and other; inner and outer; between 'wishful dreams' and reality; female and male; helplessness and control. Above all it is a process of transition between redefining oneself as child of one's parents and acquiring definition as the parent of one's own child – constituting a disorganising shift of core identity with potential reversion to narcissistic defences.

Finally, *the state of pregnancy involves duplication*. Having two people inhabiting one body is a bizarre and disturbing phenomenon. Containing within herself an 'extraneous object' yet one that is part of the self (to reverse Freud's view, 1914, pp. 89–90), each pregnant woman grapples afresh with a confusedly merged self/other concept, both imaginary yet of tangible impregnation. The symbiotic representation of two-in-one revives primordial emotions, inviting introspectiveness and interchangeable identifications with both her fetus and archaic mother of her own gestation. Captivation by the fetus as narcissistic mirror (or metaphorically speaking, by the amnion 'pool' in which Narcissus is reflected), exacerbates potential narcissistic vulnerability to boundary dissolution, with consequent breakdown or rigidification of defences in the expectant mother (and/or her partner). It is but a small step to falling in love or in hate with her or his own reflection in the baby.

Narcissistic symptomatology described by various clinicians includes illusions of perfection, grandiosity and self-sufficiency (Freud, 1914; Kernberg, 1974) conjured up to combat failure of separateness and differentiation (Rosenfeld, 1987), inferiority (Kernberg, 1974) and low self-esteem (Kohut, 1983). All emphasise lack of self-knowledge and fragile sense of self. This is manifest in incompletely differentiated self-boundaries (Mollon, 1993), destruction of separateness and confusion between inner and outer (Symington, 1993), and pathological symbiotic bonding (Robbins, 1982), often resulting in manipulative exploitation and parasitic relationships.

In this chapter I propose that defensive manoeuvres aimed at restoring narcissistic equilibrium and self-image are frequently employed by people prone to narcissistic disorders during the transitional trajectory of childbearing, which, by its very fundamental nature, threatens identity, touches on raw nerves and reactivates primal desires.

Narcissistic disturbance associated with childbearing

Narcissistic disturbances of childbearing may be triggered in vulnerable people by the following various precipitating factors:

- *Prolonged failure to conceive* in spite of an intense desire to do so highlights the illusory quality of bodily management. Repeated monthly failure constitutes a profound narcissistic injury to people intensely focused on maintaining a self-image of superiority and omnipotent control.
- *Joint dependency in reproductivity* negates the idea of self-sufficiency. Mutuality may be denied by a narcissistic male partner through phallic conceitedness and/or sexual obstructions, and by a female through delusions of parthenogenesis or the reality of self-insemination. The illusion of autonomy may be further punctured by the embarrassment and humiliation of dependence on medical assistance with conception, in cases of subfertility.
- *Conception and creating life* from within oneself enhances megalomanic beliefs, but simultaneously nausea, threatened miscarriage and general uncertainty increase awareness of one's own limited influence over the process and outcome of pregnancy.
- Reproduction of *genetic inheritance* can be cause for celebration, but when it revives unresolved early conflicts and primal scene anxieties, it may be defensively treated as an Oedipal triumph over the parents or confirmation of self-generation.
- Preoccupation with phantasies of *omni-satisfying intrauterine bliss* may reinforce aggrandised self-representations (and doubts) as bountiful provider. Similarly, regressive narcissistic cravings and overidentification with the idealised fetal state may lead to postnatal prolongation of early infantile dependence. Conversely, where projective identification prevails, disavowed dependence, contempt, punitive envy and destructiveness are aroused, and fetal abuse and/or postnatal deprivation may result.
- Terrifying *life and death responsibility* for a helpless and dependent being may result in exhibitionistic omnipotence or narcissistic sadomasochistic superiority games.
- Exposure to evocative, poignant and emotionally arousing *phenomena of infancy* provokes a lifting of infantile amnesia, increasing empathic understanding in some, or a threatened warding off of helplessness, defensive denial of emotion and distancing in others.

- Caregiving confronts parents with unbounded concrete possibilities for *vicarious enjoyment* of, and direct bodily indulgence in, sensually gratifying experiences of close contact and intimate care, thus fostering opportunities for physical and sexual abuse.
- Likewise, child care is a powerful means of replay through *active re-enactment* of internal scenarios by turning of the tables – the helpless child has now become strong parent, with the new baby cast as reinvented scapegoat or forced into playing the role of a better parent.
- In short, parenting provides rich opportunities for reliving and sharing one's *accumulated emotional experience*, a chance to invest, reinvest, guide, repay, compensate and reciprocate, and numerous opportunities for taking revenge.
- Needless to say, above all, childbearing also offers *healing opportunities* to question old versions of one's lifestory, and gain insight and increased narcissistic satisfaction by reworking one's own childhood experiences differently.

These factors, and many more, contribute to revivals of conflict in vulnerable expectant parents with consequent complex permutations of *enhanced or diminished self-esteem and/or overvaluation or denigration of the child-to-be*. Therapy during pregnancy or at the point of entry into the world of parenthood, can do much to alleviate some of the crisis:

A woman comes to see me during her first pregnancy in a state of panic. She feels very ill and is terrified of this state over which she has no control. With time, she is able to articulate her fear that she will turn out to be 'just like her mother' – seemingly a possessive, greedy and selfish woman who stopped at nothing to gain her daughter's total devotion and, indeed, during the girl's teens had threatened suicide saying: 'if you leave me, I have nothing to live for – you are my whole life.' After a bitter struggle for independence, which has involved physical separation and estrangement, the pregnant daughter now fears her internal mother emerging from within her in the guise of a baby girl, who, needy, demanding and possessive, will make irrational claims upon her. Thinking about it she feels claustrophobic, experiencing extreme annoyance with her unborn daughter. She is also terrified of falling into an abyss of uncontrollable love for the baby as her own mother felt for her, afraid that she too will be unable to differentiate between herself and the baby girl, treating the two of them as indistinguishable as does her mother with her. In addition, like many women, my patient dreads being so 'swallowed up' by the joys and duties of motherhood that her own hard-won personality will become submerged. In spite of a good marriage, unlike her mother's, my patient is afraid of becoming so involved with her unborn baby that her husband will recede into the background as her childhood father did.

She finds it very hard to tell her 'real' mother that she is pregnant – afraid that the pregnancy will be taken over and come to 'belong' to her grasping mother. When, eventually, she does tell, she lies, saying they have only just found out she's pregnant, and never mentions her therapy or contact with her midwife, dreading her mother's lifelong jealousy of her relationships with other women. With time we come to realise how crucial it has been to her mother to see herself as the centre of her daughter's world, seemingly the sole source of good things and to preserve an illusion of their symbiotic inseparableness and interchangeability in the face of my patient's growing need to keep her at bay.

In the course of time she has a son, and finds relief in her immediate sense of his separateness. Determined to maintain her own career and adult identity she encourages the cheerful little boy to occupy himself, which he does with interest. Nevertheless she is finely tuned to his needs, and through her close relationship with him also comes to have more compassion for her mother, whom she generously allows a share in caregiving. My patient continues working through many of these issues throughout the first year of his life and is able to contemplate the idea of a daughter in her next pregnancy with greater equanimity and trust in the integrity of her more solid sense of an autonomous self.

Narcissistic enactments

In most cases, overtly narcissistic perinatal representations tend to fade as awareness of the reality of the baby's individuality increases. Self-appraisal also alters as the the parenting experience unfolds, and changes incrementally with expansion of the family and birth of subsequent children. Nevertheless, an index child may remain the receptacle for positive or negative narcissistic investment or, sometimes, each of the children may unconsciously represent a particular idealised or repudiated facet of the parent (as often demonstrated in the narrative of an analytic session).

When, in spite of the passage of time, a parent cannot conceive of the baby as separate and existing independently from her or him, it becomes apparent that the baby is equated with part of the self. This non-differentiation may be consistent with a pre-existing narcissistic personality structure and habitual treatment of others as mere puppets – omnipotently controlled manifestations of his or her own influence. In other parents, it indicates prolongation or intensification of the transient narcissistic fixation triggered by the regressive pull of pregnancy and birth, in which part of the self is felt to be in actuality externalised in the form of the awaited child. This may be an overvalued good part, a split-off disparaged aspect or a disowned yet glorified destructive/dependent/demanding/insatiable, etc. property of the self which is given full play in the infant. Whichever, through extensive over-identification or projective mechanisms of fusion, invasion, possession and control, psychic boundaries between the baby and parents are negated and the infant is treated not as a person but as a personification of some aspect of the parental internal world – out there, available for all to see.

One of the hallmarks of such extreme narcissistic displacement is non-recognition of the baby/child as a person in his or her own right. This may involve selective valuation of 'special' aspects of the child, fixation on a specific age (beyond which the child abruptly loses his or her appeal and is displaced by another) or a more generalised symbiosis or impaired boundary differentiation persisting long beyond infancy. Parental enactments of protracted narcissistic fusion/confusion may take various forms at different periods of the offspring's life with more or less intense degrees of disturbance. I suggest a gradation of narcissistic displacement:

- *Doll in the box* – non-recognition of the child's sentience ('a being with no existence but what I give it').
- A more subtle *possessive symbiosis* ('You can have no needs/initiative of your own because you are me').
- *Simple interchangeability* - the unconscious parental investment of their own needs in the child ('I am feeling hungry. You must be fed').
- A joint but *competitive economic system* with some differentiation ('If she or he feeds I go hungry'). This last syndrome of displacement I refer to as a 'squeezed balloon' with an underpinning unconscious paradigm of conjoint resources – the more one has, the less available for the other.

Narcissistic representations in childbearing

In my work with pregnant women and couples I have often seen how long before the birth an expectant parent swells with gestation. Their fragile sense of self may be bolstered by exploitation of the child-to-be as a narcissistically enhancing appendage, the pregnancy itself becoming a source of exhibitionistic gratification and, later, the infant, a glorified representation of an aspect of her or his *ideal self*. Once born, although the baby is granted some separate existence, through mechanisms such as projective identification and selective reinforcement the parent unconsciously *actualises the child of his or her desire*, by selectively fostering and rewarding those very characteristics which are in accordance with the phantasy, meanwhile ignoring, disparaging or extinguishing the infant's spontaneous initiative. Such narcissistic investment may flourish in a same or different sex baby. A mother may identify her baby-self totally with her baby daughter or invest her idealised dreams of being male and penis envy in her son. Likewise for a father. Using the metaphor of carer/baby as a common balloon, as the air is displaced from one part to another, we may imagine the baby's 'true self' (Winnicott, 1960) diminishing as the parent's phantasy baby swells. ('My son's the spitting image of me – just a miniature version with his whole life ahead instead of half-gone.') The tailor-made child is destined to fulfil grandiose parental hopes.

For other parents, the wished-for baby symbolises not an idealised aspect of the self but a *messianic force* meant to change their lives dramatically, releasing hidden potentialities and blocked resources in the parent. ('Since I was little I've always known that all I needed to do was hang on until I could have a baby and then everything would come right.') As desired changes fail to materialise magically following the birth, the ordinary baby may be blamed and penalised by parental narcissistic rage for the inevitable disappointment and flatness of experience.

Alternatively, the child may be treated neither as an external self nor a catalysing object but as a *reflecting 'selfobject'* (as Kohut calls the responsively admiring source of narcissistic 'supplies'), parenting the parent. ('She's only two but so sensitive to me she can read my mind – always knows exactly what I need, not like some I could mention. . .') The baby's needs must be subordinated to recognising and meeting the adult's needs. Succumbing to these subtle but all-enveloping pressures results in infants struggling from earliest days to live up to impossible attributions to become the redeeming saviour and heal parental hurts and ancient dissatisfactions.

Yet others are *replacement children* with no right to exist of their own accord, except as inexact replicas, confused by a sense of their own reincarnation as the dead child and rivalry with a preconceived image of themselves in the parent's mind. An adult patient says:

> Visiting my parents I realised how much of the time I was seething with unexpressed rage. My mother arouses such mad, intense feelings in me – she watches me all the time and is so anxious and overinvolved with everything I do – even when I breathe I feel she'll pounce and tell me I'm doing it wrong. She makes me feel I don't know who I am or what's real or what belongs to whom. I was meant to be somebody else. Always seemed the person I am has no right to exist. I'm a husk, my liveliness scooped out by her like a mealworm. It makes me want to murder her – then I feel so monstrous for killing her off. As a tiny child I felt handcuffed to her – chained by her overprotectiveness and my guilt. She didn't talk to me but used to sigh a lot and I was convinced that her absolute anguish must be my fault. Only when I was older did I realise she was depressed, mourning my sister I never knew had existed. I was the ghost and my sister was real to her. I want to find myself but seeing how vulnerable and fragile she is I still seem compelled to do everything I possibly can to be who she wants and make up for her tragic life – and when I leave, I feel I'm taking away from her everything she needs for her survival . . .

In my consulting room, I often see (and have filmed) tiny babies living up to their carer's specific phantasy projections – anxiously monitoring the adult's responses, inhibiting crying, smiling to appease parental frustration or assuage their rage, lightening depression and seemingly making efforts to mollify and placate, enliven or subdue – tracking and producing with exquisite precision the desired reaction of the moment. Using that balloon metaphor differently – the hardworking mercurial baby droops as the stroked parent's narcissism inflates.

This competitive duality happens too when, rather than swelling narcissistically through the infant as guardian angel or external manifestation of their own internal perfection, expectant parents expand with their own *superior munificence* and the prospect of becoming a bountiful source of all goodness. The baby's function is merely to feed back gratitude and admiration, boosting parents' views of themselves as ideal providers. Needless to say, the care thus dispensed, especially when modelled upon an omnipotent figure, will tend to focus more on the parent's need to be seen to give than on what child needs to receive. In extreme cases extravagant or inappropriate care may disguise neglect, coercion or envious attacks. Through infantalisation helpless dependence may be fostered yet denounced and parental exclusivity may further isolate the child from mitigating supplies outside the family. By alternately withholding and lavishing care, the controlling parent's power grows at the expense of the child's neediness, confusion and self-devaluation.

Imminent parenthood may represent a chance not for self-expansion, but for a paring down. Jettisoned unwanted portions of the self – weaknesses and *split-off needy or damaged aspects* – are invested in the infant. The child is narcissistically exploited to highlight parental self-sufficiency or superiority while serving as a container of the parent's repudiated needs or greed. Constituting a single narcissistic unit with the child, although denying their mutuality, a parent may obtain vicarious satisfaction by actually encouraging manifestation in the infant of the disavowed characteristic, even while overtly disparaging it: 'You won't believe what a greedy brat he is – he actually wolfed down a second jar of that revolting babyfood apricot mush.'

To mothers and fathers such as these, parenthood seems to offer a narcissistically enhancing fresh start – as wise, powerful, restrained and strong – unburdened by shameful needs and despicable emotions, while at the same time expressing and gratifying these through the child. Similarly, a systemic unit may evolve with each playing out part of a destructive complex (see, for instance, the sadomasochistic–narcissistic agent–victim parent–child mirroring structure described by Gear et al., 1981). Returning to the balloon analogy, we may say that the child swells with parental expulsions.

Intergenerational patterns of narcissistic distortions are often repeated when the child, treated as *parental property*, inhibits both personal needs and resourcefulness. In some families, intricate structures interact to keep abusive patterns intact: 'I am desperate to have a baby but I feel I won't be allowed to have one' says a woman some years following recollection of a sexually abusive incident in childhood:

Sometimes it seems that the more I want a baby, the more afraid I am that I can't have it. If I take responsibility I may make it not happen – by fouling it up. As if I will somehow contrive to mismanage it at the vital point, so as to carry on cheating myself of it and feel deprived . . .

. . . My mother glosses over reality – pretending things are not happening. I feel gagged. All my life I denied myself my own truth, by allowing the illusion that my father and mother were protective and caring to govern my life. I abdicated control, gave it over to them by not speaking out as a child – allowed my truth to be manipulated by them and betrayed myself. I know I'm still susceptible to manipulation – not listening to what I know is right I allow others' more powerful views to dictate my life. This is a very important flash of understanding but it's almost trickling away through my fingers . . .

It's so hard to think that my 'sweet' mother was neglectful; that she is swayed by my father to disregard me; that in their orbit I still behave as if nothing has changed. No wonder I took tranquillisers to dampen down the truth and my real self – a lid over a seething pit of rage. My self-abuse is triggered by repetition of their behaviour. I think I enact my mother's neglect of me – can't help acting it out, as a child I fell through the gap in her perception. It's so painful to face the fact she thought she was the perfect mother but was rarely there when I needed her, and she blocked channels of communication between us. She obliterates me – if I talk about my childhood she tops it with stories of hers. But I collaborate in her image of me. . .

She owes me something but I don't know what it is. She has a claustrophobic need for me – it's as if *only one of us can thrive – either her or me*. And even now I feel I must protect her at my expense, hold onto my secret and not speak out because I'd destroy her life's illusions by telling. . .

Having a baby of my own would be so restoring but it's so hard to believe I can become pregnant because any strong life force in me is countered by prohibition . . . torpor, a great desire to sink into nothingness and go nowhere. It's similar to the fog I'd switch into in my childhood to blank out knowledge that I'd been abused.

['A fog that also blanked out knowledge of your own capacities.']

Yes, my capacities were always disparaged at home. Superficially it's easier to not know them but more damaging. It's still problematic how to suddenly generate my own self-esteem out of thin air. When I do it feels like 'nervy energy' – as if its been suppressed for too long . . .

When what I have called the *'doll in the box' syndrome* is taken to extremes, not only is the newborn's individuality denied ('Tabula rasa'), but the baby's humanity too ('If anyone ever asked me a question my mother replied for me.'). There is little recognition of the child as a 'going concern': to use Winnicott's felicitous phrase, a sentient being with an inherent core of liveliness. The child is merely an appendage of the parent. This syndrome may range from a situation where, when not being actively looked after, the child ceases to exist – obliterated from the oblivious parent's mind, to the flip-case, of constant heightened anxiety stemming from disbelief in the baby's capacity to survive as an independent entity when the mother or father sleeps or for a moment ceases to think of, or think for, 'it'.

As we shall see from a clinical example, for a child being constituted within the orbit of such a caregiver's unconscious representations, internalisation of the self as a parental appendage or introjection of the adult's lack of faith in natural viability or prohibition of initiative has the effect of doubt about having an immutable separate existence. The child may find it impossible to free him- or herself from the parental phantasy. Conversely, a parent living out the situation of displaced narcissism becomes depleted by projective identification and lacks direct agency unmediated through the phantasy child.

Internalisation of parental narcissism

Many of the above ascriptions of parental narcissism are absorbed into the forming identity of a child to become unquestioned features of her or his own self-image. Frequently this leads to an unresolved confusion between – *the internalised Other; projected parental narcissism; the child's self-experience; and the introjected narcissistically distorted image of the child's self as perceived by the caregiver*. As we have seen from examples above, disorders resulting from displaced parental narcissism become highlighted when, deciding to have a baby of his or her own, the grown-up child has to confront his or her own narcissistic vulnerability in the struggle for individuation. Many seek therapy at this point hoping to achieve internal separation from narcissistically disturbed parents with a hope of reproducing her- or himself differently.

Surveying my adult patients past and present, I realise how frequently I have come across a family situation in which children have grown up as a parental appendages or 'dolls in a box', with so little sense of their own capacities or talents and reasonable entitlement to wishes, desires and fulfilment that they cannot conceive of their life as their own. With some this takes the form of undefined passive waiting for '*one day*' when they will be fed/rescued/played with/compensated for past deprivation by new parental figures seen to have untold resources. Others may anticipate a *magical event* (such as graduation, marriage or the birth of a baby), after which the clock of their life will finally start ticking (see 'messianic force' above). For yet other young people (in whom the 'squeezed balloon' syndrome predominates) parental needs eclipse awareness of their own. This may take the form of unfulfilling accomplishments intended to satisfy parental expectations or, in families emphasising parental deprivation, the child's acute preoccupation with mother's or father's early hardship or manifest suffering is coupled with a grandiose determination (often later relocated in professional life) to compensate – to rescue the victims, repair the damage and '*make good*' the deficit irrespective of personal sacrifice.

The same individual may oscillate between both stances of *passive waiting* and *active altruism*, and these become prominent features in their intimate, therapeutic and work relationships outside the family, too. In common, the inertia of the first stance and the sacrificial endurance of the second, promote 'stuckness' in life and an inability to move on. What both stances share is an unconscious belief in *systemic interconnectedness of the parental/child pool of vital resources*. This underpinning conviction may only become evident during the course of very long analyses.

For example, for many years a patient had felt devastated each weekend of the analysis, feeling she vanished even to the point of seeing no reflection in the mirror. She often became disoriented and agoraphobic yet afraid of being on her own, feeling she ceased to exist unless somebody else was there to acknowledge her. In time she came to express her experience as gradual awakening from seeing her world only through her mother's eyes, and living as part of her mother. It was some years before shapes and colours took on vivid clarity and her body stopped alternating between kinaesthetic experiences of feeling dead or hypersensitively receptive, ravenously hungry or inexplicably bloated, enormous or very little. The sense of fragmentation that followed non-existence gave way to increasing awareness of herself as an ongoing entity, but it was many more years before she could become secure in her conviction of having resources of her own which made her less dependent on the goodwill of others for her very existence. It was at this point that she began being able actively to enjoy being on her own. Later, she was able to contemplate the possibility of cultivating under-used artistic talents and for the first time began employing her considerable initiative in her job on her own behalf, rather than allowing herself to be exploited by others. With a tentative but increasing sense of entitlement she became able to choose, buy and discriminatingly furnish a flat of her own, and poured a great deal of effort and thought into what has become a flourishing garden. Finally, she found it not inconceivable that she might find a respectful partner and even have a baby.

I shall bring a few verbatim excerpts (from this hitherto dutiful daughter in the eleventh year of analysis) from the concluding period of her lengthy and very fruitful analysis, which illustrates some of these gradual changes and her increasing awareness and consolidation of them:

> I don't want to hear my mother's voice on the phone it seems to get inside me to make me do things on her behalf . . . I know she feels a victim but she won't do anything to help herself, just relies on me to do it for her. It's always been difficult to be what she wanted me to be to please her – had to be exactly her way – neither too much nor too little. So many times I've been taken in by believing that her concern was for me but when she speaks to me I become not a person but some part of her that must act for her, as her, and I realise she only ever noticed my doing anything for her when it stopped. . .
> She gave me so little but always behaved as if she was the best mother in the

world and I was never allowed to have anybody else or anything of my own, not even my grandma, or my own friends, or clothes I chose, or even drawings I made.

Again, some sessions later she touches on both aspects of the competitive maternal economy I've termed the 'squeezed balloon' and the 'doll in the box' syndrome:

My mother can't let herself have something pleasurable – its more painful for her to have than not because it will not be there all the time. But, she seems to envy anything I've got – my flat, my job, even my hair – as if she feels I have it all and won't give her any. All my life since I was tiny I've spent so much of my time worrying about her and curtailing myself and doing the Right Thing and not really living, barely living – as if I was part of her, not feeling entitled to breathe by myself as if I didn't deserve to exist. She wanted a special baby, an ideal little her, and was so cross because all she got was a screaming brat. I felt so terribly responsible as if I'd spoilt it all for her by coming along. . . I'm not meant to be except as an extension of her – I'm meant to get things for her and be her. It's so incredibly deep, I even wore clothes like her in my 20s as if had to make amends for dressing differently and having wanted a boyfriend. . .

I had so very little sense of myself . . . so disengaged from myself. Only recently in the analysis I've had some idea of making a space inside myself for my babies – whatever kind they are – but even now as soon as I want something for myself, I begin hearing these voices in my head telling me what I'm not allowed – like Mum taking the bowl away when I wanted to lick it or making me feel wicked for daydreaming. And it still feels outrageous to say 'no' – nobody will like me if I do what I want. . .

Some months later, watching a friend and her baby interact, the same woman is pained as she comes to realise with hindsight some of the unconscious dynamics in her own childhood and the internalised effects of lifelong treatment as a doll-baby:

My mother has no idea, and never has had, about a baby or child's needs – it's so mixed up with her own needs that she thinks knowing what her needs are is sufficient and a baby's needs are just the same. She expected so much from me and nothing from herself – felt that whatever she did was great . . . and for long periods of time seemed to forget about me as if expected me to hibernate or bring myself up . . . she was blind to me and I was blind too, to me, to her, to her blindness. I had to blind myself to her shortcomings and make looking after her my young life's priority.

My father too was envious of everything I had. There not only was no encouragement to achieve – they expected me not to move on – and seemed resentful that I didn't stay as I was. I felt guilty even going to school, or away to camp, to university . . . Last night I dreamed I rented a baby to learn how to change nappies – kept bringing it out of its plastic bag to show people. I so want to broaden my life, but still worry about getting tired, running out, exhausting resources, having nothing left. I want to do more and more, not less, but have to overcome fear of getting swallowed by things or defined by others.

In the following weeks her rage and confusion begin to pour out as never before:

> I feel savaged and destroyed and torn apart limb by limb, hair by hair, undermined and made to feel like rubbish . . . no relief or escape, not even in sleep. . . My mother treated me as useless, as soon as I hear her voice now I feel such hatred I want to smash her silly little head against the wall. . . . She was gripped by mad forces, whenever I disagreed or said anything that suggested I had a mind of my own I was treated as vile. On the weekend I collapsed into bed and stayed there – what a relief to accept I can feel vulnerable and weak and have limitations, don't have to be superwoman for my mother or stick it out stoically or conquer anything.
>
> This is the biggest shock of my life – beyond speech or frantic state – the idea that I don't have to stick with my family forever, that I have a choice. It seems very important to acknowledge how shocking it is – the shame and guilt about my family and how wrong it felt not wanting to stay with them, as though I should have stuck there forever. . . I'm reeling with the shock of letting something go – a chunk of the past – and facing how few of my needs were ever met . . . I feel burned out.

Weeks later, having rediscovered her capacity for productive work, speaking about her hopes for a relationship, my patient is afraid that I will think she is 'going on'. Laughingly, she imagines I'll say: 'Oh God! here she goes – got a right one here!' Of her mother she says:

> Just by the way she breathed I knew she couldn't stand it if I wanted something . . . yesterday, I saw a beautiful nightie in a shop –but asked myself: 'what's wrong with a T shirt and old pair of leggings'. I could hear my mother's voice: 'gosh! what a waste of money!' – but it was lovely, all frothy and lacy and satiny – a pinnacle of luxuriating femininity. I think I'm telling you because I want to hear reassurance that I deserve it – that everybody does, that its not greedy or self-indulgent to want something beautiful – as if I'm not sure of that whole aspect of womanhood – being a sensual woman and allowed to enjoy it and have fun and be proud of it and even to enjoy being pregnant and having a baby, not as a sneaky little secret perversion but living it openly and fully. With my mother it was like a compulsion. She sacrificed herself to stay with my father. She said she had me 'cos after a few years of marriage you're supposed to have a baby – but I think really she wanted one to keep hold of my father because she never really had him – like she wants to get hold of her grandchildren now in a hungry, desperate way like a starving person wants bread, as proof to wave at the world, to fill herself up, get rid of the emptiness and to show she's got loads, plenty. That's why I always have to try to get away from her – I sensed what she was doing and felt it was dangerous for me although I wasn't aware of my feelings – of anger, distress, a backlog of rage at being dismissed and undervalued. *I was never there in my own right* – and any sign I was, was a threat to her and she showed in millions of ways that it was not acceptable to her, even that I've got my Dad's features not hers. *She wanted me to be a replica but as she's not acceptable to herself – she's doomed to be dissatisfied. . .*

As we see, after many years of having little sense of herself as a separate viable entity rather than the servicing auxiliary of her mother, gradually through a prolonged analytic process of emotional self-discovery, my patient has painstakingly built up internal solidity and awareness of her entitlement to want, and a capacity to use her own resources on her own behalf. This is manifest in her sense of confidence: 'Everything's it's proper size – the "Grand Canyon chasm" has shrunk to a hairline crack and when things go wrong I don't panic and automatically think "I can't do it".' She has consolidated her sense of existence:

> . . . I'm still a bit afraid of analytic breaks – on the first days I turn to jelly. But then I get better. Before part of me seemed to disappear as if everything stopped while you were away and had to wait 'til you got back. I used to get sick or hibernate, now I just get on with my life'.

She has a greater sense of self-definition ('The balance has shifted. I'm not yearning to be anywhere else. I'm not defined by what I do – work is not a substitute for life outside and I'm not pursued. I used to feel responsible for everything, now I can garden or read for pleasure. . .'), agency ('I've learned that any endeavour involves effort and that crucial battles take place out there in reality. I feel really pleased making my own decisions, making something of my life rather than inwardly groaning. It feels more adult – I'm no spring chicken – and I feel entitled to make choices, neither reckless nor overcautious.') and involvement in the present ('Always felt a nagging, gnawing discomfort of being unable to find my place as a child – always wanting to be grown up as if being a child was something to be ashamed of. Although I still haven't got kids, a husband and house – I feel in tune with time – neither waiting for the future nor wishing time away – just being in it.'). And, finally, she has developed a healthy narcissism ('Phantasy used to feel mad, dangerous, would lead to a muddle of disappointing empty reality – now it seems an enjoyable way of loving oneself, interconnected with aspects of reality that mirror my growing. I feel full of myself – not 'too big for my boots' but entitled and deserving.').

I will end with an expression of my patient's feelings of optimism as she reaps the harvest of her long hard work of becoming herself, which seems to say it all:

> . . . now, I consistently have a feeling I've had flickers of at times in my childhood – richness, colours, light, smell, lush and golden like the fields at the end of the day at the height of summer when it can't get any riper and there's a glow on everything – an intensity of beauty almost painful to see — a sense of something realisable, within my grasp . . .
>
> Its been such a fragile difficult thing to get to trust myself – taken so much work to make myself trustworthy. I can only do things in my way for my reasons which nobody else does know and only I can find out. A year ago I felt not all done. Amazing that the timing is so precise. Is it like that for everybody? . . . Now I feel full, responsive, teeming with life.

Postscript

On the day I had allocated to discuss with my patient my use of this material (but before I raised the issue), she began talking of a thought she'd had that morning in relation to a childhood memory triggered by last night's telephone discussion with her mother, followed by a dream of being pregnant with twins. Her thought was simple – but she had never had it before. That perhaps her grandmother, an avid gardener, whom my patient had loved dearly, emulated and always defended, *had* been cruel to her mother, who seemed never to be able to tell when she was being abused. In fact, at times, mother turned things 'upside down', seeing abuse as 'value', as when her son, my patient's brother, made extortionist demands on her which she did her utmost to meet. Associating to the 'twins' in her dream, my patient now says:

> For as long as I remember I always wanted twins; I wanted to be a twin and in all my relationships behaved as if I was one. It is only since I've lived on my own that I've become aware of the joy of just being myself, my own special person without the need of a twin to understand and interpret for me, be with me and give me things. There's a pleasure in doing things for myself directly, feeling pleasure in my own body, being me, away from the madness of tied-interdependence. I used to feel even my body didn't belong to me . . . it's difficult to understand because it operates at such a deep level when you're not yours, but I think it's why I felt I couldn't have a baby of my own and why I was so afraid of having my body taken over by one.
>
> I think the dream is upside down . . . *Perhaps my grandmother treated my mother as a twin* – an abused bit of herself, and filled her up with awful projections of her own. It was so hard for my mother to get away from her mother, she seemed to feel so guilty, in the wrong, expected to produce something as if she should have been able to make everything alright. I always believed it *was* my mother's fault but perhaps something between them fucked her up – she was my grandmother's rubbish bin, as I've felt at times I've been for my mother.

Thus, she has come full circle, compassionately establishing herself as a link in the female chain of mothers and daughters, each of whom, unable to process her own 'rubbish', has deadeningly projected it into the twinned–caring–daughter-self. And depleted by jettisoned self-value, each has then cultivated and sought narcissistic validation from an idealised demanding male. However, my patient's newfound healthy narcissism enables her to extract herself from life-by-externalised-proxy, the land of puppeteers and dolls, to enjoy her own life. Leaving behind her the Siamese-twinship of a co-terminus 'balloon' economy in which there is not enough to go round and what one has must be squeezed out of, or owed to, another, from her vantage point as a whole separate person she can now use her strong sense of agency to provide for herself. And far from looking into her mirror and seeing no reflection or the blurred image of her mother's phantasy or her own compliant echoing response, she now clearly sees her own live face, the reality of which she can contemplate with interest and increasing self-knowledge.

References

Badcock C (1994). *PsychoDarwinism – The New Synthesis of Darwin and Freud*. London: Harper Collins.

Fairbairn WRD (1952). *Psychoanalytic Studies of the Personality*. London: Tavistock

Freud S (1914). On narcissism: an introduction. *The Complete Psychological Works of Sigmund Freud*, standard edition, vol. 14, pp. 67–102. London: Hogarth Press.

Freud S (1915). Thoughts for the times on war and death. *The Complete Psychological Works of Sigmund Freud*, standard edition, vol. 14, pp. 273–302. London: Hogarth Press.

Freud S (1920). Beyond the pleasure principle. *The Complete Psychological Works of Sigmund Freud*, standard edition, vol. 18, pp. 3–65. London: Hogarth Press.

Gear MC, Hill MA, Liendo EC (1981). *Working Through Narcissism – Treating its Sadomasochistic Structure*. New York: Jason Aronson

Kernberg O (1974, 1980, 1984). *Internal World and External Reality – Object Relations Theory Applied*. New York: Jason Aronson

Klein M (1946). Notes on some schizoid mechanisms. In: *The Writings of Melanie Klein*, vol. 3. London: Hogarth Press, 1975

Kohut H (1977). *The Restoration of the Self*. Madison: International Universities Press

Kohut H (1983) Selected problems of self psychological theory. In: JD Lichtenberg, S Kaplan (Eds), *Reflections on Self Psychology*. Hillsdale, NJ: Analytic Press.

Mollon P (1993). *The Fragile Self – The Structure of Narcissistic Disturbance*. London:Whurr Publishers.

Raphael-Leff J (1986). Facilitators and regulators: conscious and unconscious processes in pregnancy and early motherhood. *British Journal of Medical Psychology* 59: 43–55.

Raphael-Leff J (1991). *Psychological Processes of Childbearing*. London: Chapman and Hall (reprinted 1992, 1993, 1994).

Raphael-Leff J (1993). *Pregnancy: The Inside Story*. London: Sheldon Press.

Raphael-Leff J (1995). Reproductive narratives – some inside stories of pregnancy and parenting. In: C Clulow (Ed.), *Partners Becoming Parents*. London: Sheldon Press.

Robbins M (1982). Narcissistic personality as a symbiotic character disorder. *International Journal of Psycho-Analysis* 63: 457–73

Rosenfeld H (1987). *Impasse and Interpretation*. London: Free Association Press.

Symington N (1993). *Narcissism – A New Theory*. London: Karnac Books.

Winnicott DW (1960). Ego distortion in terms of True and False Self. In: *The Maturational Processes and the Facilitating Environment – Studies in the Theory of Emotional Development*. London: Hogarth Press, 1965

Winnicott DW (1967). Mirror role of mother and family in child development. In: *Playing and Reality*, Chapter 9. London: Penguin Books.

Chapter 8
Narcissism in ageing

ANNE ZACHARY

> The most difficult task in life for us all is to face our own inexorable ageing. Lumping old people together, out of sight, in conditions of tedium and dislocation which we would find intolerable ourselves, is our way of avoiding the inevitability.
>
> *Bennett (1994)*

What is it that prevents our being able to address more easily the natural process of ageing with its ultimate end-point in death?

Theories of narcissism develop as psychoanalysis ages to be almost a century old itself and help to understand why this task is so difficult. Laplanche and Pontalis define primary narcissism as 'an early state in which the child cathects its own self with the whole of its libido', and secondary narcissism as 'a turning round upon the ego of libido withdrawn from the objects which it has cathected hitherto'. This sets the scene in its Freudian context and more recent ideas can then be included later as they are relevant.

This chapter will focus on the probably universal secondary narcissism which prevents easy ageing, retirement, relinquishing of authority, etc. How difficult this is to write about here when belonging to a profession in which one does not qualify until the age of 35 at the earliest, and in which the eminent figures to whom we aspire are in their 70s, 80s and sometimes even 90s. What a comfort this is from a narcissistic point of view; what a worry it is when challenging personal defences and striving to maintain integrity. Pearl King (1980) has commented on the experience of growing old as often one of shame, humiliation and narcissistic injury.

There is a healthy narcissistic force in everyone and the adolescent will be primarily preoccupied in relationships with the question: 'Will they like my body?' This comes into focus again with ageing and old people can have a similar preoccupation, although this is not necessarily a conscious phenomenon. It will extend from the ageing woman's wish to colour her hair or the ageing man's combing over his bald patch to remain recognisable as the younger version of themselves, to the much older person struggling not to drop food down his or her clothes as an almost total preoccupation. Although this can be seen as basically narcissistic, of course it is equally a measure of dignity and self-preservation. But it follows the definition of secondary narcissism in that, in an economic sense, relationships with others lose that investment of libido which is increasingly required to maintain the self.

The level of the narcissism and whether it is healthy or pathological will depend, to start with, on early development and whether the individual is only caught up with 'How beautiful I am', or whether it extends right into the identity of the self and back to the fundamental question of 'I am'. This developmental process can become a regressive phenomenon in later life. Noel Hess (1987) in his paper 'King Lear and some anxieties of old age' draws also from clinical consultations with elderly patients. He illustrates that, with increasing age, there can be a terrifying anxiety about total helplessness which, as we are enlightened by Shakespeare, can be experienced as a narcissistic injury. Here ageing parallels primary and secondary narcissism in that there might be absolute or relative dependency and a loss of that part of the self which contains narcissistic injury, especially where there is illness or dementia. He calls the defence against this anxiety a narcissistic tyranny, defending against any knowledge of one's own misery. History also shows us the common occurrence of powerful leaders who become increasingly autocratic, even despotic, as their youth fades and there is an ever-growing desperation to maintain their position. Staying with great literature, we can empathise with the young and beautiful Dorothea in George Eliot's *Middlemarch* (1985) who is assured of a secure future financially on the death of her much older husband Casaubon, but, in a cruel codicil to his will, only as long as she does not remarry. As he has a fair idea that this is already on the cards and that it involves his younger, penniless rival, Ladislaw, himself already entitled to, yet barred from, inheriting from Casaubon in his own right, this is indeed tyranny of the self acted out.

With increasing age, for the individual in whom there has always been a problem about narcissistic injury and the need to defend against it, the damage to identity and the assault on the object will be the more severe. When there has been a lack of awareness at any developmental stage (childhood, latency, adolescence, adulthood, mid-life), it makes the ordinary journey through maturity to old age more difficult. Quite often people panic at the first middle-aged death in their peer group. This can be seen as a sign of avoidance of ageing and mortality issues. They can only see themselves as for-ever young. Perhaps old people are banished in the painful way described in the opening paragraph of this chapter because (1) their carers are afraid of what they themselves might become or (2) they are having to defend themselves against being used as narcissistic extensions of elderly people who need them in order to function and who would rage like Lear without that investment.

Narcissism is, however, universal and only pathological in degree. Healthy narcissism can be a life-giving and positive defence and women, in particular, have the opportunity that if they can negotiate the menopause constructively, they will take on a new lease of life in their 'third age' with an inbuilt developmental advantage. Women analysts in the middle years of this century – Helene Deutsch (1984), Therese Benedek (1950, 1960) and Karen Horney (1939) – wrote about women's experiences around the menstrual cycle and the menopause advocating that they were at an advantage to men in preparing for later life. Benedek (1960) researched women's dreams which differed at various stages of the monthly cycle – exciting and constructive at ovulation, forbidding and destructive premenstrually.

Reaching into the unconscious, this advantage that women have goes beyond the usually quoted cardioprotective capacity of oestrogen. The aim is to prevent a regression and instead to achieve further developmental maturity. All their lives women have been preparing unconsciously for the loss of their fertility in the monthly menstrual cycles, most of which end in the failure to conceive. (Of course this is usually of great relief and with the availability of contraception, more often than not nowadays, consciously arranged that way.) In an unconscious sense it is linked closely to the biological aim of pregnancy and it is a loss. Literally, there is a loss of blood. How fundamental in terms of potential for life this is. At the menopause this monthly signal that fertility has failed for the moment ceases and instead there are no more bleeds indicating that fertility has ceased in a final way. (Again, hormone replacement therapy transcends and postpones this but I am linking the biological framework to that of the unconscious.) Therefore, because of the monthly biological reminders, the loss of fertility does not have to come as a total shock, and so does not leave women without potential or motivation and at risk from early deaths.

A Jungian analyst, Ann Mankowitz (1984), while pursuing this positive line of thought really takes up the narcissistic element involved in women's ageing. Of particular relevance here is a chapter she calls 'The fear of knowing'. In people with normal eyesight, a deterioration is often noticed after the age of 40. It is interesting that the deterioration in eyesight generally happens around the same time as the menopause. Although it is obvious that both are symptoms of the body's decline in middle age, failing eyesight is rarely, if ever, mentioned in relation to the change of life. Mankowitz suggests that there might be an investment in not seeing something that would be unbearable to see. Narcissistically, this could include the visible signs of ageing. Nature does try to be kind. As one gets older and more wrinkled, the eyes get dimmer so that on looking in the mirror the wrinkles cannot be seen so clearly and so an illusion of youthfulness can be maintained.

Victoria Hamilton (1993) has compared Oedipus and Narcissus, pointing out that Oedipus wanted to know whereas Narcissus avoided looking and knowing, the narcissistic's fear par excellence. From a developmental stance this is the classic difference between those who negotiate the pain of the Oedipal situation successfully and those whose narcissistic injury would be too great if they fully recognised that mother had her own partner.

Elliot Jacques (1965) looks at the situation relating to ageing for men. Instead of their having a menopause they acknowledge a mid-life crisis. Men who do not negotiate their future death with a period of reflection, even depression in their 40s, however, will be at risk of sudden death, for example, on retirement.

Most useful in looking at these processes is carefully selected case material from day-to-day clinical work. I will present here, for contrast, examples of a single woman preparing for retirement who had treatment and who probably avoided suicide in doing so, and a male perpetrator seeking treatment who in the end was unable to face such self-scrutiny. Both of these individuals (the former deeply neurotic by way of her isolation, the latter by way of his perversion) are extremely narcissistic in their developmental psychopathology and especially in their negotiation of increasing age. These cases come from my practice in the NHS setting where analysts can work as psychotherapists, adapting psychoanalytic theory in an effective way, in order to reach individuals for whom psychotherapy would otherwise be unavailable.

Miss A

Miss A agreed to a brief period in psychotherapy. She was a single and childless woman who was selfless but resentful. She had had a dedicated career in a helping profession and was renowned for her sweetness and capacity to give. She was horrified by her depression and suicidal feelings at this time in her life. She was 49 and had a strong family history of early death. Her two brothers had died in their 50s from cancer and heart disease, and her mother had died at 55 of heart disease. Her sister had married and had children but she had had depression at the menopause. Miss A was the youngest and, having always felt as a child that she was the one whom they all relied upon to fetch and carry because her parents were ageing by that time, she went into a career which allowed her to continue in her characteristic manner. She had formed a serious relationship with a man who did not want to marry. She had thought long and hard about living together, but decided that what she needed more than anything was her own security, so she bought a place of her own and later broke off with him. Her warm, coping exterior shielded her deep resentment about not having anyone to care for her, but she cried a lot during our first interview. She tended to project her vulnerabilities into the people for whom she cared during her work.

She felt deeply ashamed that she was having problems and not much aware that she might need and be able to use help herself.

She did decide, however, to continue in treatment. Much of the material focused on her difficulties managing her flat and she was preoccupied with an upstairs balcony from which water was flooding down into it. It was feared that the structure was not up to specifications and she was waiting for the freeholder to investigate. It seemed to illustrate her experiences within her body because she was having night sweats and floods of tears, the latter both alone and while with me. The balcony represented the 'roof over her head' and this was significant in terms of her fear of what I would do, that I would leave her with her roof off and spilling out all over with her tears with such a brief period of therapy.

When she was able to acknowledge some of her resentment towards her family, towards the man who had not married her and towards me in the transference because I was not going to go on seeing her, she left treatment feeling internally stronger and able to face her retirement years with a more positive and consciously self-oriented outlook.

Mr B

Mr B is a man in his 70s with a lifelong history of paedophilic phantasies and compulsive acting out. In recent years he has had several convictions and in a counselling setting appears to have shifted slightly in that he is able to feel depressed and openly ashamed about his urges and offences. In this frame of mind he sought psychotherapy saying that he had probably only a few years left and he would like to work on why he has had to do such things and to try to come to terms with it before he dies. Most important, he hoped it would prevent his acting out any more in the future.

His father died when he was 14. His mother died 20 years ago and he remembers her warmly. He was married although it is long time since he divorced and it is known that he also abused his own children. Born into poverty, he was evacuated to the country as a result of the war. Although he remembers being well looked after during this time, he was a victim of sexual abuse by two older children at the age of 11 years. He was threatened with violence if he told anyone.

Following on from this, although he married and was successful in a career, he compulsively repeated the abuse involving young boys of about the age that he had been himself, whenever he could, apparently without thought, guilt or remorse. In this way he was able to maintain some sense of psychic comfort, fragile although it would have been. Humiliated by charges, imprisonment and public knowledge of his misdemeanours, he had moved from a position of total mindlessness about his behaviour with no internal inclination to control it, to a position of some suffering with the wish to change. It was at this point that he was referred for psychotherapy.

There was no immediate vacancy and by the time one arose he had returned to work part-time. Seeing him again I recognised the polite well-dressed exterior. In no uncertain terms he told me straight away that he had no intention of taking up the offer of psychotherapy at this stage. He felt that he had got himself back on his feet, that to wait had been of no help to him at all and that, as far as he was concerned, the offer was as many months late as the wait had been long. He said also that, in addition to his feelings about this, he was no longer depressed.

Here is a patient who, in retrospect, can turn down an offer of the help he so desperately needed. The question that is raised in such a severely narcissistic personality is, however, whether, if the treatment had been offered immediately or even after a shorter wait, he would have been able to take it up then or in any event sustain it. I believe that he was too narcissistic really to contemplate an exploration of his defences and that, had he been offered immediate treatment, he would have declined at the beginning or dropped out very soon rather than face his real feelings of guilt, shame and depression. He could not bear the narcissistic damage that facing up to his internal world would represent for him. Although he put this in terms of having been able to make the internal changes necessary by himself while waiting I did not feel as optimistic. His refusal to take up the offer of treatment was a defensive cover to the wound he would have experienced if he were actually to be confronted with his deep-rooted problems. Khan (1960) has emphasised that such individuals cannot acknowledge a need for the other and have to provide their own solutions.

Discussion

Going back to Victoria Hamilton (1993) and the difference between Oedipus and Narcissus, although neither of my clinical examples can be said to be homosexual, I think that Miss A's avoidance of partnership is evidence of her ongoing attachment to her mother and Mr B's paedophilia is evidence of his pain in losing contact with his mother so early. He has a perversion but Miss A's inclusion here underlines that although all those with perversions will be narcissistic, not all narcissistic disorders are perversions.

Narcissism is an integral part of the ageing process, a universal and necessary phenomenon achieving dignity and survival until life can be sustained no longer, which in itself is another topic. We need to distinguish healthy narcissism in ageing, with its importance both personally and professionally, from ageing and narcissistic disorder. In disorder, lifelong tendencies such as those that Miss A and Mr B exhibit (with the latter being more severe than the former who may arguably not even fall into the category of disorder) become accentuated at the mid-life stage and may or may not be alleviated by treatment. Willingness to be treated becomes the realistic factor and with Mr B the retreat from this possibility was in itself an example of narcissistic defence as he hid behind the professional delay making the situation seem like a failure in the object rather than a distancing stemming from his own vulnerabilities.

References

Benedek T (1950). The climacterium: a developmental phase. *Journal of the American Psychoanalytic Association* 19: 1–27.

Benedek T (1960). The organisation of the reproductive drive. *International Journal of Psycho-Analysis* 41: 1–15.

Bennett C (1994). Ending up. *The Guardian* 8 October.

Deutsch H (1984). The menopause. *International Journal of Psycho-Analysis* 65: 55–62. [First translation into English of a chapter of *Psychoanalysis of the Sexual Functions of Women* (1925). P Roazen (Ed.). Freud's Press.]

Eliot G (1985). *Middlemarch*. London: Penguin Classics. Originally published 1871–2.

Freud S (1914). On narcissism. *The Complete Psychological Works of Sigmund Freud*, standard edition, vol. 14, pp. 67–104. London: Hogarth Press.

Hamilton V (1993). *Narcissus and Oedipus*. London: Karnac Books. Originally published in 1982 by Routledge & Kegan Paul.

Hess N (1987). King Lear and some anxieties of old age. *British Journal of Medical Psychology* 60: 209–15.

Horney K (1939). Feminine psychology. In: *New Ways in Psychoanalysis*. New York: Norton.

Jacques E (1965). Death and the mid-life crisis. *International Journal of Psycho-Analysis* 46: 502–14.

Khan M R (1960). Clinical aspects of the schizoid personality: Affects and technique In: *The Privacy of the Self*. London: Hogarth Press, 1974.

King P (1980). The life cycle as indicated by the nature of the transference in the psychoanalysis of the middle aged and elderly. *International Journal of Psycho-Analysis* 61: 153–60.

Laplanche J, Pontalis JB (1983). *The Language of Psychoanalysis*. London: Hogarth Press.

Mankowitz A (1984). *Change of Life: A Psychological Study of Dreams and the Menopause*. Toronto: Inner City Books.

Chapter 9
Narcissism and bereavement

HAZEL DANBURY

The grief that has no expression in tears makes other organs weep.

Henry Maudsley, quoted by Joyce McDougall (1994)

Introduction

To consider the implications of the narcissistic patient already in psychotherapy when she or he becomes bereaved, it is necessary, first, to examine 'normal' bereavement. It is particularly important to have a thorough understanding of the common manifestations of grief in our culture, as many of them would be seen as abnormal were it not for the fact of the bereavement. If a patient is already in therapy there is a danger of seeing as pathological those reactions that are commonly experienced and are known to be within the normal range of responses by the bereaved. These might include hallucinations, somatic disorders, delusions, as well as narcissistic regression with increasing dependency, vulnerability, anxiety, insecurity and extreme withdrawal symptoms. The therapist needs to guard against seeing a general pathology in the narcissistic patient, resulting from the bereavement. The therapist's task is to isolate areas where the narcissism impedes and prevents the process of grieving, working to free the patient from its obstructing elements in order to be able to continue grieving.

Levin (1993) points out that all psychotherapy is dealing with loss, as every change in life involves loss (see also Winnicott, 1965).

Since World War II theories of attachment and loss have been a subject for research on both sides of the Atlantic. Research has shown that the way in which attachments are made in infancy affects the way they are made in adult life. This has a direct bearing on the way in which losses of all types are experienced. A thorough knowledge of the literature relating to attachment and loss is crucial to any study of bereavement. It is even more essential if the bereaved has a narcissistic personality, because it is out of primary narcissism (Freud, 1914, p. 90) that anaclitic attachment develops. Whether one subscribes to instinct theory or to the theory of object-relations, primary narcissism is the precursor to the development of the ability to form attachments and, subsequently, mature love relationships.

In his paper 'Mourning and melancholia', Freud (1917) distinguishes between mourning, which is normal, and melancholia (chronic depression) which is not. Although the 'symptoms' may appear to be the same, Freud suggests that:

> . . . melancholia is in some way related to an object-loss which is withdrawn from consciousness, in contradistinction to mourning, in which there is nothing about the loss that is unconscious . . .
>
> *Freud (1917, p. 245)*

Psychotherapy is not indicated for the latter, however distressing it may be. To offer psychotherapy to all bereaved people conveys the message that grieving is pathological. In his commentary on Freud's paper, Levin (1993) observes that the mourner must withdraw all strands from the lost object, which bind him or her, re-introjecting the projected bad part-objects, in order to 'decathect' (let go), introjecting the projected good ones, and become free to reinvest in another object. As Allingham (1952) puts it:

> Mourning is not forgetting . . . it is an undoing. Every minute tie has to be untied, and something permanent and valuable recovered and assimilated from the knot. The end is gain, of course. Blessed are they that mourn, for they shall be made strong, in fact. But the process is like all human births, painful, long and dangerous.

However, Levin does quote Freud's slight shift in attitude after the death of his daughter, Sophie:

> . . . we . . . will never find a substitute. No matter what may fill the gap, even if it is filled completely, it nevertheless remains something else.

In bereavement there is inevitably an element of regression, as there is in any traumatic experience which leaves the subject feeling not in control of important life events (Spitz, 1946a,b), and thus particularly vulnerable and helpless (Seligman, 1976, 1992). A certain amount of narcissism in the bereaved is therefore to be expected and is perfectly normal; it is no indication of the need for specialised help. As with many experiences of the newly bereaved, narcissistic regression does not have to occur, but it is perfectly normal when it does. Donne (1572–1631) knows this when he says 'any man's death diminishes me'.

There are many fluctuating and oscillating emotions through which the bereaved may pass on the journey towards achieving acceptance of the death and readjustment to the new circumstances. The theory of stages implies the successful negotiation of each before one can pass on to the next. Research has shown this is nonsense. Even the concept of phases is too rigid. There is a wide variety of experiences and fluctuating feelings, all of which come within the range of 'normal' grieving, but not everyone encounters all of them by any means. Also, the length of time taken to grieve varies according to the individual's particular history. Indeed, grief may be triggered off unexpectedly at any time in the future, but each succeeding time it is of shorter duration. However, because the narcissistic person hangs on to the lost object in order to control and attempt to preserve it, the task of grieving is made harder and may never be near completion. The bereaved person usually regresses in the course of grieving in different ways a number of times.

In his paper 'Mourning and melancholia' Freud (1917) was writing at a time when death was becoming a taboo subject in Western society. It remained taboo from the end of World War I (as a result, among other reasons, of the need to repopulate quickly) until comparatively recently. By the time Gorer was writing about the subject in 1965 (p. 113), he noted that:

> ... mourning is treated as if it were a weakness, a self-indulgence,
> a reprehensible bad habit instead of a psychological necessity,

with bereaved people being referred to psychiatrists if they were unable to hide their grief. It is noticeable that early writing and research into the subject is by psychiatrists. Grief had come to be seen as abnormal.

Bereavements that are most likely to reactivate narcissism include the following:

1. The death of a parent
2. The death of a spouse
3. The death of one's children.

The experience of mirroring is central to these attachment relationships (Bowlby, 1980; Pines, 1984), because they are modelled on the earliest relationship. Steiner (1990) reminds us of the part played by projective identification in the creation of narcissistic objects. Part of the mourning process is becoming separate from the lost object, and to do this successfully the bereaved person must be able to recognise 'what belongs to the object and what belongs to the self', and to let go of the former, while owning the latter.

It is only if the pain of this is too intolerable and the bereaved becomes stuck in a state of narcissism during the grieving process, or if the bereaved has a narcissistic personality, that psychotherapy is indicated (see Raphael, 1984).

Theories of attachment, loss and narcissism

Attachment and loss

According to the empirical research of Bowlby (1980) and Ainsworth (1982, 1991), there is now a substantial amount of evidence supporting the importance of the primary attachment relationship in the individual's ability to form subsequent attachments. This is not to imply that a good or poor primary one forms the blueprint for all others, but that if failure in the first one goes unrecognised and therefore uncorrected, subsequent ones are likely to repeat the pattern formed by it.

Others who have contributed to the research on attachment and loss include Spitz (1946a,b, 1965), a psychoanalyst whose studies of infants in hospital and orphanages in North America led him to develop the concept of learned helplessness, later taken up by Seligman (1976); Bowlby (1951, 1969, 1973, 1980); Ainsworth (1982, 1991); Main and Weston (1982); Weiss (1982, 1988); Parkes and Weiss (1983); Marris (1974, 1982); Parkes (1991). These have all researched empirically, whereas others, for example, Klein (1975a) and Winnicott (1965, 1969, 1971) have contributed by rigorous clinical observation. Whatever the specific terminology used, there is general consensus that the infant passes through primary narcissism to secondary narcissism before developing a mature, altruistic, secure attachment. Insecure attachment can result in the person remaining narcissistic, because narcissism is essentially a problem of separation. On the basis of her 'Strange Situation Test' (p. 233) in her research, Ainsworth (1982) lists three types of attachment to the primary figure:

1. Securely attached infants – they cried less on brief separation and showed pleasure in re-uniting.
2. Insecurely attached infants – these cried more and showed rejecting behaviour on re-uniting.
3. Ambivalent infants who showed clinging and avoidance behaviour.

The insecurely attached person finds it difficult to separate from the attachment figure: from infancy, his energies have been absorbed in constantly checking that the mother (or substitute) is there. He is unable to forget self, is anxious and cannot feel free to be creative. The securely attached child knows and trusts that his mother is available. He does not even have to think about it and he is thereby free to explore and move around. Secure attachments lead to the ability to separate and become independent and creative. Insecure attachments lead to stultified development, including narcissism.

Parkes (1994) points out that the word 'attachment' in point (2) is neutral; an attachment bond may be positive, negative or have elements of both. Thus, in the research outlined above, the first step towards establishing an affectional bond is made with a secure attachment (Ainsworth, 1991). She further defines 'affectional bond' as 'a relatively long-enduring tie in which the partner is important as a unique individual, interchangeable with none other'. She emphasises that affectional bonds are not relationships, because they 'are characteristic of the individual but not the dyad'. The bond may be between mother and child, lovers, child and parent, other kin or friends. Affectional bonds give security, care giving and provide a sense of self-worth.

A bereaved person who has a history of insecure attachments is likely to have difficulties in working through the process of grieving, in letting go of the deceased and in adapting to living a new life. It may be that a securely attached person, able to make a permanent and loving relationship, finds the process of grieving less problematic than someone with a stormy relationship who nevertheless has a strong attachment. Many divorced people are caught in this, a situation made worse by the society's surprise at the one's grief, on the death of the other, and because of the continued existence of belief in the myth that the greater the love, the greater the grief. The evidence also supports the theory that the number and type of losses experienced in the past, and the extent to which they were made manageable, influence the way in which an adult reacts to a major bereavement (Parkes, 1991).

Thus in assessing whether or not a bereaved person may need psychotherapeutic help, it is important to understand his or her particular history of attachments and losses. This has become a central issue in compiling the list of risk factors in recovery from bereavement. According to Parkes, Bowlby's (1969, 1973, 1890) work on *Attachment and Loss*:

> . . . remains the chief statement of attachment theory and a model of the successful development of a scientific paradigm. The relationship a child develops with his mother . . . forms the starting point for later relationships.

(The convention is followed here of using the word 'mother' to stand for the main nurturing carer.)

Narcissism

When the death of a loved one occurs a return to the paranoid–schizoid position (Klein, 1975a,b) is almost inevitable because a narcissistic wound is opened, possibly with accompanying persecutory phantasies. If this state persists, it obstructs the grieving process. The loss of the mirroring object produces narcissistic rage. When the bereaved remains in a state of narcissism, or has never managed to progress beyond it, and the world is still seen as revolving around the self, she or he continues to feel persecuted by the loss of the mirror-object. Levin (1993) also comments on this saying that:

. . . Klein casts light on the origins of the capacity to mourn and on the developmental arrests that impede mourning.

While this situation persists, grieving for the loss of the object cannot
take place (Steiner, 1990). Narcissistic persecutory rage impedes the
internalising of the valued parts of the lost object, the taking back and
owning of the projected parts and the casting out of the parts without
value.

Joyce McDougall (1994) makes the link between narcissism in
bereavement and that in psychosomatic disorders. The narcissistic
mother who does not allow her baby to separate, but keeps him in a
state of fusion with her, may be producing someone who in later life may
fear the psychic pain of grief so much, that unconsciously somatic disorders are substituted. She maintains that all psychosomatic disorders are
child-like attempts to cope with or prevent the anguish of mental pain;
there has been a breakdown in symbol formation (Segal, 1957; Klein,
1975a,b). She refers to language that clearly alludes to the link, although
the attempt to ward off intolerable psychic pain by somatisation is
preverbal and becomes unconscious. Common examples include
sayings such as 'choking with anger' and 'crushed by grief'. McDougall is
talking about persistent somatisation in order to avoid psychic pain.
Again, the normality in any bereavement of producing psychosomatic
symptoms must be stressed, because this allows the pain of grief to be
made manageable and coped with gradually.

Dr Jurgen Moltmann (1994) maintains that the whole of our Western
society is a narcissistic society, full of relief mechanisms, trying to love
without grieving and blocking off the grief; this results in intolerable
depression. As Freud (1917) observed, the narcissistic ego feels abandoned and betrayed. Moltmann points out that narcissistic love is love of
the object in order to enhance the self, and the object becomes a possession (my wife) and not a love for the object itself. For adequate grieving
to take place, the narcissistic elements of love have to be shed. Those
who really love have a part of themselves dying with the deceased and
have to integrate the dead part within themselves and get into a new
relationship with the dead person (Bowlby, 1980) so that reinvestment
in life can take place (in Marris's terms, to find a new meaning in life).
Moltmann reminds us that, although all love is not narcissistic love,
nevertheless it all contains an element of enhancing belief in self-worth
and esteem.

Brenman (1985, p. 425) also believes somatisation to be used to
avoid facing one's own psychic reality and to avoid a breakdown:

> The narcissistic organisation is of paramount importance. The pretence of
> being loving and friendly is *not* designed to achieve a loving relationship, but
> to be the falsely adored object of love and to triumph over so-called loving
> objects who are then despised and annihilated.

There are many different relationships in which the death of one member leaves others bereaved. A major problem if one of the bereaved feels narcissistically wounded is that this person sees him- or herself as the only bereaved person, failing to recognise that others, in different relationships to the deceased, are also bereaved and are therefore grieving. This has been a frequent problem for adolescent children who have lost a parent, for example, and the widowed parent fails to recognise his or her right to grieve for the loss of a parent.

A few examples of narcissistic bereavements in different relationships follow, but these are by no means exhaustive.

Narcissism and death of a parent

The death of a parent is very different for different people; it has separate significance according to the age of the bereaved person. To someone in middle age who has an old parent, the death may be a sad occurrence, but not necessarily an occasion for a great deal of grief. The original intense parental attachment is likely to have been withdrawn from the parent many years earlier and become invested in the partner. Sometimes, however, the parent and child have never separated, so that the death of the parent is a severe narcissistic blow to the child, who may be middle-aged.

One such patient found that her dependence on her mother had left her ill-equipped to cope with life, in spite of her having her own family. She could not imagine how she would cope with her own children without her mother. In the transference, the therapist became the withholding bad breast, denying her sustenance.

How the infant or small child reacts depends largely on where she or he is in his or her emotional development. The amount of adult understanding, support and alternative nurturing being given can be very important here, because the child may remain stuck in a state of wounded narcissistic omnipotence, preoccupied with self and unable to grieve, or she or he may be helped through this by understanding and aware carers. It has already been stated that regression is normal in traumatic circumstances, whatever the age of the bereaved person, and that this should not be forgotten.

It is usual for all children to see themselves as responsible in some way for the fate of those whom they love and on whom they are dependent. The Kleinian theory of the phantasy of the infant's belief in the power of his destructive rage is confirmed to the child by reality when a parent dies. Too often, those who take over the care are unaware of this and the conviction of culpability remains, haunting the child with guilt. If still an infant, the child is left in a state of omnipotence with a belief in the potentially destructive power of his rage and other negative feelings.

The problem of the bereaved adolescent or young adult has only recently received attention. In concentrating mainly on researching into the effects of widowhood, the fact that children are also grieving for the loss of a parent may become overlooked. In relation to narcissism, the focus has been largely confined to the effect on the adolescent of narcissism in the surviving parent. The child may be seen by the parent as a support who is expected to take over the role of the deceased parent. This is a common narcissistic regression, made worse if the surviving parent is not merely regressing because of trauma, but is truly narcissistic. The role reversal, where the child becomes the parent, is then maintained through this dynamic. Sons and daughters who find themselves in situations of this sort may have to face denial of their need to grieve. Many find themselves in therapy later in life, with delayed grief to work through. It is fortunate that the prognosis is good for them (Worden and William, 1991), whereas it might not be so good for the narcissistic parent.

> 'I never had an adolescence.'
> 'I had to become a responsible adult overnight.'
> 'I had lost a parent, but was not recognised as being bereaved.'
> 'No one thought I was grieving, too.'

These comments were made by people who had suffered a parent's death during their adolescence, but whose grief was not acknowledged by the surviving parent.

One adolescent who was expected to take over the father's role did not feel free to grieve until after the death of the other parent. He was conscious of holding back and felt very isolated because of the lack of others' awareness of his own need to grieve. Fortunately subsequent bereavements can provide the opportunity of working through any previous unresolved grief at the same time as the current one.

In families where the dynamics are reflected in succeeding generations – a common occurrence – both the surviving parent and the adolescent may be narcissistic, in which case they will be able neither to support the other nor to appreciate that the other is also bereaved.

Narcissism and death of a partner

Narcissism is the precursor to all attachment relationships, and the position from which all other relationships develop. The primary attachment relationship is normally the model for future relationships, particularly lasting partnerships and, as such, essentially contains within it a substantial degree of narcissism, which is not necessarily pathological. This is not to deny the healthy, adult, sexual component in the relationship, but it is important to recognise that the loss of a partner can inflict a narcissistic wound on the bereaved so great that it may not pass during the grieving process, but remain to complicate the grieving.

Whether or not the death is expected, untimely or one of a number of multiple deaths, it is always a shock when it occurs. Feelings of helplessness and loss of control of one's own life may occur, and it is important to find some area in life where the bereaved may quickly regain a sense of control. This may prove very difficult with the narcissistic patient, whose preoccupation with self gets in the way of grieving for the lost one as well as preventing adequate social readjustment. Normal regression, produced by death, can result in the bereaved feeling rejected and abandoned by the partner, as if being deserted for another – which, in a sense, is so. However, whereas this is usually one of the transitory feelings experienced by the widowed, it may remain permanently there in the narcissistic patient, if untreated, so that resentment and anger obstruct grief. The bereaved partner feels as if the spouse died deliberately to distress the one who is thereby widowed. It is difficult for this person to form other, secure relationships without help from psychotherapy.

When dealing with a widow's bereavement a therapist, who had not previously recognised her patient as being narcissistic, commented:

> I stopped treating this patient. What was the point of continuing when she was stuck in depression, reiterating that she would never get over what it had done to her?

Another patient refused to view the body of her husband, who had died very suddenly and unexpectedly, in spite of her children begging her to. She was so identified with the lost object that she avoided anything that would help her to accept his loss. Instead, she demanded that her therapist attend the funeral; she made the therapist hold the knowledge and reality of the death instead.

Narcissism and death of a child

> He only does it to annoy,
> Because he knows it teases.
>
> *Lewis Carroll (1832–98)*, Alice in Wonderland, Chapter 6

To lose a child is often considered to be the worst of all bereavements. Miscarriages, abortions and stillbirths are now recognised as bereavements, frequently causing similar reactions in the mother as the death of a child. In his paper 'On narcissism', Freud (1914, p. 91) says:

> Parental love, which at the bottom is so moving and so childish, is nothing but the parents' narcissism born again, which, transformed into object-love, unmistakably reveals its former nature.

Gender differences, whether innate or culturally determined, frequently make it impossible for the parents to comfort each other. For example, the mother may want affection without sexual contact, whereas the father may find sex comforting. She wonders that he can think of such a thing at a time like this, while he is bewildered, with his efforts at comfort rejected. Thus each rejects the other and feels rejected by the other.

Add narcissism to this and there is frequently a divorce. As with other narcissistic bereaved, the narcissistic mother may become stuck in severe depression or in constant somatisation, as substitutes for being able to face the pain. Preoccupation with what this death has done to her feelings of self-esteem and self-worth create obstacles to the process of grieving.

The quotation from *Alice in Wonderland*, at the start of this section, shows graphically how the narcissistic parent may react to the death of her infant.

The therapist was trying to work with the patient towards her allowing her infant to begin the process of separation, as she was obviously struggling for some independence and autonomy. The patient could only experience her as an extension of herself, still fused with her, when suddenly the child died. The patient's overwhelming grief carried with it rage and also a sense of outrage that the child could do this to her. She was unable to extend any compassion to her husband.

There is likely to have been a role reversal, once again, between the narcissistic parent and the older dead child. If only one parent is narcissistic, the suffering of the other can be made more acute by having to cope with the partner's preoccupation with self. Unfortunately, this is the type of response frequently held by the narcissistic patient, who is still emotionally in an exclusive two-person relationship, not having been able to negotiate to transition to a three-person (and thus a hundred also) relationship; she or he sees the world still revolving around her or him, so that any bereavement is experienced as yet another form of attack, this time by the deceased. Narcissism can lose one sympathy and attract the accusation of trivialising the death by demanding the centre stage and reacting as if the death is a personal attack.

In the case of an adult child's death, there may be a narcissistic surviving parent of the deceased, whose narcissism ensures that no one else is seen as also being bereaved. This can result in problematic grieving for more than one person.

The following example shows how a narcissistic takeover can surface, triggered by the trauma of death.

One widow, who was with her husband at home when he died, had allowed his parents to stay overnight. This meant that her own mother and her children had to spend the last night of their father's life with a friend round the corner. As he died that night, the children were not there with him at his death. In the morning the new widow went round to her friend's house to tell her mother and her children that he had died. She returned to find that her mother-in-law had told the funeral director to take the body away, which he had done and she had made the arrangements for the funeral. She could not understand why her son's widow and children were so distressed. She thought it quite unsuitable for the children to have wanted to be with him in his own home when he died, as well as it being irresponsible of their mother to have encouraged them when she (their mother who was now the widow) had no right to do so. This mother-in-law could not accept that it was she who did not have the rights, position and status of the nearest relative and chief mourner. She could not accept that she did not have the right to take over organising, nor could she accept the widow as a member of the family, let alone the real chief mourner, nor could she accept that anyone was bereaved except herself. Not having separated herself from her son, now dead, she was unable to recognise the new family, her son's wife and children, but was keeping him bonded with the original family. His death provided the circumstances for the mother to act out long, life-standing phantasies of her son's body belonging to her 'naturally'.

Raphael (1984) systematically goes through deaths of different members of the family and friends, together with the possible different experiences, responses and relationships of the bereaved members. When discussing the death of children, for example, she divides them into different groups, according to their various ages and stages/phases of development.

Working with the narcissistic bereaved patient

In working with narcissistic and borderline states, Hedges's (1983) work on 'listening perspectives' can be extremely useful in helping the therapist to know in which state the patient is at any particular time.

One narcissistic patient was so identified with his therapist that, for a long time, his attendance at sessions was patchy. Sometimes he was 45 minutes late, sometimes he was early and sometimes he never came at all. Never did he show any awareness of this behaviour or apologise, because he experienced the therapist as being always with him. Another patient showed her narcissism by flying into a towering rage when she saw the therapist go into the consulting room after the patient had arrived and was in the waiting room. She believed that the therapist ought always to be in the consulting room:

What if I suddenly need you?

It is now accepted that the reactions to bereavement are not those of a steady progression towards something called 'recovery' which is usually measured by general health and social functioning, but that responses are a series of fluctuating feelings covering a wide range of

reactions. There is no such thing as a 'normal' length of time for grieving. Humans are infinitely variable and influenced by their past which
they carry with them; thus grieving is very individual and will take whatever time it takes. There is no such thing as recovery from bereavement;
one learns to live with it and through it, gradually adapting to the
changed circumstances. This can be difficult enough for the bereaved
who do not carry the additional burden of narcissism, but to those who
do, a difficult and even more lonely path lies ahead, as the preoccupation with self is in the way of mourning the loss of a loved one. The
bereaved always becomes stuck at the point of 'what this has done to
me'.

If grieving is too painful to face, then it is likely to be displaced, chan-
nelled into chronic depression (Freud, 1914; Levin, 1993; Moltmann,
1994) or a succession of psychosomatic disorders (Levin, 1993;
McDougall, 1994). It is in situations such as this where psychotherapy
with the bereaved can be of great help, but family, friends, general prac-
titioners and bereavement counsellors need to know this. Too often they
do not, so that the problems of those most in need of psychotherapy go
unrecognised and therefore not referred, unless the individual refers
him- or herself.

Levin (1993) summarises Freud's and Klein's contributions to the
understanding of narcissism and bereavement. Freud emphasises the
importance of withdrawing all emotional investment in the lost object,
in order to be able to reinvest in a new one. Klein traces the origins of
the development of the capacity to mourn, which cannot take place
while still in the paranoid–schizoid position. It is the:

> . . . task carried out by working through the depressive position. Mourning
> through reparation enabled by gratitude both consolidates the depressive
> position and makes further mourning possible . . . Those who have not
> reached the depressive position lack the capacity to mourn . . . the stronger
> the ambivalence toward the lost object, the harder it is to mourn.
>
> *Levin (1993, p. 262)*

> . . . early mourning is revived whenever grief is experienced in later life.The
> most important of the methods by which the child overcomes his states of
> mourning, in my view, the testing of reality; this testing process, however, as
> Freud stresses, is part of the work of mourning.
>
> *Klein (1940, p. 344)*

References

Ainsworth M (1982). Attachment: retrospect and prospect. In: Parkes CM, Stevenson-
    Hinde J (Eds), *The Place of Attachment in Human Behaviour*. London: Tavistock.
Ainsworth M (1991). Attachments and other affectional bonds across life cycles. In:
    CM Parkes, P Marris (Eds), *Attachment across the Life Cycle*. London: Routledge.
Allingham M (1952). *The Tiger in the Smoke*. London: Chatto & Windrush.

Bowlby J (1951). *Maternal Care and Mental Health*. London: HMSO. [Abridged version (1953). *Child Care and the Growth of Love*. London: Penguin.]

Bowlby J (1969). *Attachment and Loss*, Vol. 1, *Attachment*. London: Hogarth Press, 1984.

Bowlby J (1973). *Attachment and Loss*, Vol. 2, *Separation, Anxiety and Anger*. London: Hogarth Press.

Bowlby J (1980). *Attachment and Loss*, Vol. 3, *Loss, Sadness and Depression*. London: Hogarth Press.

Brenman E (1985). Hysteria. *International Journal of Psycho-Analysis* 66: 423–32.

Carroll L (1832–98). *Alice in Wonderland*, Chapter 6. London: Penguin.

Danbury H (1995). A study of the effectiveness of bereavement counselling. PhD thesis, University of London.

Donne J (1572–1631). No man is an island . . . In: *Devotions and Sermons*. London: The Nonesuch Press, 1962.

Freud S (1914). On narcissism. *The Complete Psychological Works of Sigmund Freud*, standard edition, vol. 14, pp. 67–102. London, Hogarth Press.

Freud S (1917). Mourning and melancholia. *The Complete Psychological Works of Sigmund Freud*, standard edition, vol. 14, pp. 243–58. London: Hogarth Press.

Gorer G (1965). *Death, Grief and Mourning in Contemporary Britain*. London: Cresset Press.

Hedges L (1983). *Listening Perspectives in Psychotherapy*. New York: Aronson.

Klein M (1940). Mourning and its relation to manic-depressive states. *The Writings of Melanie Klein*, Vol. 1, p. 355. London: Hogarth Press, 1975.

Klein, M (1975a). *The Writings of Melanie Klein*, Vols 1–4, London: Hogarth Press.

Klein, M (1975b). Mourning and its relation to manic–depressive states. *The Writings of Melanie Klein*, Vol.1, p. 344. London: Hogarth Press.

Levin JD (1993). Slings and arrows: narcissistic injury and its treatment. In *Loss*, Chapter 4, pp. 251–67. London: Jason Aronson.

Main M, Weston D (1982). Avoidance of the attachment figure in infancy: descriptions and interpretations. In: Parkes CM, Stevenson-Hinde J (Eds), *The Place of Attachment in Human Behaviour*. London: Tavistock.

Marris P (1974). *Loss and Change*. London: Routledge & Kegan Paul, 1986.

Marris P (1982). Attachment and society. In: Parkes CM, Stevenson-Hinde J (Eds), *The Place of Attachment in Human Behaviour*. London: Tavistock.

McDougall J (1994). *Grief and the Psychosoma. First Keynote Lecture*. Fourth International Conference on Grief and Bereavement, Stockholm.

Moltmann J (1994). *On Grief and Melancholia in Modern Society. Second Keynote Lecture*. Fourth International Conference on Grief and Bereavement, Stockholm.

Parkes CM (1991). Attachment, bonding and psychiatric problems after bereavement in adult life. In: Parkes CM, Stevenson-Hinde J, Marris P (Eds) *Attachment across the Life Cycle*. London: Routledge.

Parkes CM (1994). *Attachment and Bereavement. John Bowlby Memorial Lecture*. Fourth International Conference on Grief and Bereavement in Contemporary Society, Stockholm.

Parkes CM, Weiss RS (1983). *Recovery from Bereavement*. New York: Basic Books.

Pines M (1984). Reflections on mirroring. *International Review of Psycho-Analysis* 11: 27–42.

Raphael B (1984). *The Anatomy of Bereavement*. London: Unwin Hyman.

Segal H (1957). Notes on symbol formation. *International Journal of Psycho-Analysis* 38: 391–7, 1995.

Seligman MEP (1976). *Helplessness*. San Francisco, CA: WH Freeman.

Seligman MEP (1992). *Helplessness*, 2nd edn. San Francisco, CA: WH Freeman.

Spitz R (1946a). Hospitalisation: a follow-up response. *Psychoanalytic Study of the Child* 2. Quoted in Spitz (1965).

Spitz R (1946b). Anaclitic depression: an inquiry into the genesis of psychiatric conditions in early childhood. *Psychoanalytic Study of the Child* 2. Quoted in Spitz (1965).

Spitz R (1965). *The First year of Life*. New York: International Universities Press.

Steiner J (1990). Pathological organisations as obstacles to mourning: the role of unbearable guilt. *International Journal of Psycho-Analysis* 71: 87–95.

Weiss SR (1982). Attachment in adults. In: Parkes CM, Stevenson-Hinde J (Eds), *The Place of Attachment in Human Behaviour*. London: Tavistock.

Weiss SR (1988). Loss and recovery. *Journal of Social Issues* 44(3): 37–51.

Winnicott DW (1958). *Through Paediatrics to Psychoanalysis*. London: Hogarth Press.

Winnicott DW (1965). *The Maturational Processes and the Facilitating Environment*. London: Hogarth Press.

Winnicott DW (1969). *The Family and Individual Development*. London: Tavistock.

Winnicott DW (1971). *Playing and Reality*. London: Penguin.

Worden J, William J (1991). *Grief Counselling and Grief Therapy*, 2nd edn. London, New York: Tavistock/Routledge.

Part III
Clinical Aspects of
Narcissism

Chapter 10
The search for a primary object: making and breaking in the treatment of narcissism

JUDY COOPER AND NILDA MAXWELL

Introduction

It is well known that Freud was never very enthusiastic about the therapeutic effects of the analytic process. And in Freud's view the narcissistic patient could not really benefit from psychoanalytic treatment as it stood. Anna Freud (1976) was also basically sceptical about the widening therapeutic scope of psychoanalysis. She felt:

> . . . that classical analysis should remain within its original realm of the neurosis, except for exploratory excursions. In a 1976 paper, Anna Freud wrote along these lines: our psychoanalytic understanding of these severe disorders has far outstripped our capacity to help them by analytic therapy; what the ego has done to itself during development can be un-done by the ego in analysis – but what has been done to the ego by early deprivation or trauma can only be healed by a modified approach.
>
>

AS Couch (1987, unpublished paper,
'Anna Freud's adult psychoanalytic technique')

Indeed, as Anna Freud remarks, there is a discrepancy between analytic theory and practice. Our theoretical understanding of infant development has grown tremendously and we now understand the nature of and reasons for severe disturbance, whereas clinical work is more arduous and random. As we know, these deeply disturbed patients do form a transference relationship both with the healthy and ill parts of themselves. However, Freud (1914) was all too aware of the narcissist's 'unconquerable resistance' which adds to the analyst's perseverant work undertaken with the psychoneurotic, because for the narcissist there is a constant need to attack the therapeutic relationship. For these patients, analysis can become a way of life, both for support and to attack: 'Such patients may need to go on in analysis partly in order to have a libidinal relationship to attack' (Rosenfeld, 1987, p. 22). Attack can take any form: from utter contempt to complete withdrawal, and the analyst can be made to feel ignored or despised. In our view, the aim of analytic treatment for these patients should be to provide an unbreakable 'container': a link that is strong enough to survive the repeated attacks on it, thus providing an experience of primary attachment which can be internalised.

The narcissistic patient

What demarcates this category of patient is their despair and sense of futility (Bollas, 1979). As they cannot internalise anything – nothing can feed, be digested or metabolised – their lives feel permanently empty. An example of this is a highly intelligent patient aged 52 years. He has spent his whole life feeling a sense of futility, unable to use his gifts or allow any of his therapies, over the years, to help him. As Glasser (1992) remarked: 'They cannot use reality.' This patient's isolated life shows clearly how this type of disturbance leads people into 'avoiding anxiety by avoiding contact with other people and with reality' (Steiner, 1993). One can feel this wholesale avoidance in the transference: 'the analyst has to carry the despair associated with the failure to make contact' (Steiner, 1993).

The personality of this type of patient is often marked by an extreme degree of splitting with fragmentation of affects, high expectations to receive, which explains their permanent feeling of disappointment, and a reluctance to give because they would feel depleted (Kernberg, 1977).

The narcissistic patient pushes ruthlessly in search of a primary object (Balint, 1968; Bollas, 1979). Hence the 'narcissistic transference' (Kohut, 1971) is different from the ordinary transference neurosis, because it involves a need for the revival of archaic objects rather than the instinctual investment of Oedipal conflicts. The fact that these patients are constantly on a search could explain why they change analysts, trainings, studies, jobs. These changes are often preceded by high achievement. They often display a sense of great urgency about their quest, and their frenzied search for an object can appear more in keeping with the behavioural profile of mania with its ingredients of triumph, control and contempt. To give an example, the patient we have already mentioned is always quoting his previous analysts. After almost 2 years of therapy he still reports his weekend happenings filled with destructive attacks on his treatment. This is a repeated behavioural theme of his; even in a 1-hour assessment with a consultant some years ago he managed to enrage him with his manic contempt for psychoanalysis.

It is not unusual for these patients to have come from another analysis and ours will not be their last stop. They feel as though they are in transit in the consulting room unless they find a perfect fit with their analyst. It is as if they are on 'a somewhat manic search for health' (Bollas, 1979). Another trait of these patients is that they cannot tolerate any recognition of separateness between self and object. This would lead to feelings of intense anxiety about dependency (Rosenfeld, 1965). They feel most comfortable in a merged state. On the other hand, they are consumed with an intense, often unconscious hostility against the primary object, and this can lead them into a repeated cycle of destruction and search.

Theories of primary attachment: proximity and connectedness

> ... when for any reason mother fails to be a steady source of satisfaction the transformation of narcissistic libido into object-libido is carried out inadequately
>
> *A Freud (1954)*

These sorts of disturbances are built over a long time: 'when object relationships continue to be unsatisfactory during the succeeding years of early childhood' (Fairbairn, 1956). Khan's (1963) concept of 'cumulative trauma' refers to this fact. Along this line of explanation, the vulnerability to traumatisation is also mentioned as important (Kohut, 1971). Winnicott spoke in terms of environmental failure or impingement and the different kinds of response to impingement.

Environmental failure can take many different forms: obviously there can be the reality of an actual loss of mother's presence; then there can be the complete lack of empathy (a neglectful, remote or abandoning mother); defective empathy (seducing mothers who lead a child into believing that he or she is mother's special object); or the over-empathic mother (intrusive and controlling). This last category has been stressed by Glasser (1992) in his concept of the 'colonising pre-Oedipal mother' who allows no space for father. Even if one admits that the actual external situation is irretrievable, through direct observation of children and through the analysis of adults, we find that there is some common agreement as to the importance of how the environment works on intrapsychic life.

Perhaps the oral component of attachment has been over-emphasised in theories such as Melanie Klein's. Bowlby (1971) says that to equate good breast and good mother could be somewhat limiting. Bowlby studied mother–child proximity in terms of an infant seeking attachment and he observed that proximity often takes precedence over feeding, even in states of hunger. Winnicott (1953, 1958), when he refers to mother's breast, includes the whole technique of mothering as well as the actual flesh: it is possible for a mother to be a good-enough mother using a bottle for the actual feeding. Vitally important conditions of motherhood are for Winnicott (1948) that 'she exists, continues to exist ... is *there* to be sensed in all possible ways' and that 'she loves in a physical way, provides contact, a body temperature, movement and quiet according to the baby's needs'. The fact that she also provides food is placed fourth. Thus, it would seem that the presence and continuity of the mother, and the provision of contact and warmth, are previous to oral needs and their satisfaction. The infant is born with nutritional provision for a few hours. We can say that placenta resources last on the nutritional level more than, for example, on the thermic level. Indeed, as Kohut (1971) points out, in relation to the need for warmth, narcissistic individuals have an enduring difficulty with regard to self-regulating their temperatures, and they depend largely on others for this function.

So what is the experience that this sort of patient lacks? What are they longing to receive? The answer would seem to be just the right degree of connectedness. The fact is that the mothers of these very disturbed patients have generally been there, but without providing contact: they were not responsive.

The concept of connectedness refers to the essential fact which guarantees life preservation after birth. After birth, it is essential to restore human proximity. The human infant needs connectedness to maintain the interuterine set of resources, both biological and psychological, in the outer world. Proximity to mother or her substitutes becomes gradually less urgent as the child grows.

The narcissist's need for a point of anchor to take him back to a time before the primary catastrophe happened is clear, that is, to a time before there was any question of loss or environmental failure where needs were not met. The need for constant change represents another unconscious hope of retrieving the original safety, however fleeting that was. Sometimes this place of safe attachment seems to have been before birth, in the womb when the baby was connected to the placenta. Or, it could come from the time when mother was active in the infant's caretaking as a 'transformational object': 'able to metamorphose his entire internal and external world' (Bollas, 1979). So, the feeling of connectedness is like being able to have both a good internal object and a good external reference point.

The external anchor point is represented by the stability and regularity of the treatment and any small shift of progress is noteworthy. For example, the aforementioned patient managed to get his rent reduced and also to go for some musical weekends which provided a break from his uneventful, monotonous, predictable, lonely existence. These small positive movements, away from the aridity of his usual life, allow us to hypothesise that something in his inner world was being repaired.

Analytic provision

As these patients are looking for ideal containment and an absolutely perfect fit of understanding, they are highly intolerant of any frustration.

The provision of an 'intermediate space' (Winnicott, 1971; Nissim Momigliano and Robutti, 1992) where experience can be shared and the analyst can offer the patient the possibility of a link with a primary object is of utmost importance to the treatment.

The analyst should, however, be wary of falling into the trap of pursuing the quest for a symbiotic object which this type of patient is so adept at presenting. For females, this longing for merger often takes the shape of wanting to identify with mother through marriage and babies whereas the male may not want this as he perceives it as engulfment. Although increasingly encouraged culturally to do so, his biological endowment does not allow merger except in a more sexualised form. For women, pregnancy and babies, especially in the first year, allows them to re-live the symbiotic experience. The dangers of living out this symbiosis for both sexes can be very damaging (perpetuating the cycle of inadequate parenting) and, in fact, Grunberger (1989) is explicit in his summing up that for this band of patients, both male and female, the principle of parenting in its reality is just not active.

It would seem that these patients require an openly warm attitude from the analyst with a reasonable degree of involvement, rather than a more neutral medical model. This attitude has to include the uncompromising provision of goods, freely given and with no expectations in return. These patients are in the position of children forever. Hence some gratification through shared experience is very relevant for them. And alongside this a careful dosage of interpretations. The main point of interpretations, quite often, is to show a patient that he has made contact with us and been understood. The right blend of these components would seem to facilitate some progress. Even the expectation of recovery could become viewed as the analyst's wish imposed, as a burden, on the patient. As these patients have the ability to provoke strong emotions in the analyst – they involve one – the analyst should be alert to this unconscious longing for merger which is always present.

As this group of patients has had such early environmental disturbances, they constantly need to re-enact the scenario of merging and breaking. Thus, if for any reason analysts fail to maintain their patients' feeling of connectedness with them, patients will almost certainly react by going into a 'malignant regression' (Balint, 1968), or with some other form of omnipotent narcissistic attack. This pattern can be extremely exhausting for the analyst.

The analyst's willingness to be found and used as an archaic object has been associated with his degree of expertise. Lomas (1987) suggests at least 10 years of clinical experience. However, this also depends on the availability of the analyst's time and energy: Little (1985) had to wait her turn to regress with Winnicott. Perhaps an analyst can only cope with one or two patients of this sort at a time.

Exhaustion is a normal component of early infant holding, but gradually the infant's satisfied needs lead to a decrease in their demands.
However, with this sort of patient the analyst must be ready for a taxing
and exhausting time, with very meagre results. A different scale of
measurement is required – one's mental microscope has to be adjusted.
Neurotics may feel a sense of fear and concern that they have exhausted
their analysts, although often this is a correct perception in narcissistic
patients because of their incessant and excessive demands (Rosenfeld,
1987).

Altogether these tremendous pressures and demands on analysts
could lead them to act out in terms of their giving real provision to their
patients (money, food, etc.) which could aggravate the symptoms
(Freud, 1909; Rosenfeld, 1987). Sechehaye (1951, p. 140) makes this
precise point calling it 'symbolic realisation' when she offers her
disturbed patient the apples: '. . . it is not the apples themselves which
count but the fact that it is the mother or her substitute who furnishes
them'. However, Sechehaye emphasises that the pre-condition for this to
take place is that: '. . . the patient had to be connected emotionally to the
being who gives' (Sechehaye, 1951, p. 140). It is in the maintaining of
this connectedness that some of the main problems arise.

Impasse

One of an analyst's main tasks is to realise when the patient is stuck.
Impasse is usually an indication that something in the analytic situation
needs to be changed. Different authors emphasise different things, but
on the whole there is consensus that the analyst must re-examine his or
her view. In fact, although, previously, breakdown in the treatment of
narcissistic patients was thought to be inherent in treating such
disturbed people, today there is a growing trend which explains impasse
in terms of treatment error and puts the responsibility on the analyst
(Nissim Momigliano and Robutti, 1992).

Impasse can show itself in so many ways. The most extreme manifestation is in premature termination of treatment. However, it can show
itself in other difficult ways such as negative therapeutic reaction, transference psychosis and symptoms such as hypochondria. Beneath these
different expressions of impasse lies the compulsion to revisit the original environmental void which has left its scar. Indeed, this is exactly what
Kohut meant by 'narcissistic injury', Winnicott by 'environmental failure', Balint by 'basic fault', Khan by 'lack of mother as a protective
shield', Bion by 'unreliable container' and Rosenfeld by his description
of 'the infant turning away from the breast with hostility'. In all these
various conceptualisations, there is a difference in emphasis between
the Independents who stress the importance of the environment, and
the Kleinians who concentrate on the infant's role. Thus, the Indepen-

dents feel that it is the failing environment that leaves its destructive mark, whereas the Kleinians believe it is the infant's 'destructive envy' that wreaks its own havoc. Both schools would agree that the patient resists exploration and rejects recognition of the original fault in order to uphold his idealisation of his primary object. As Rosenfeld points out:

> When a containing relationship breaks down . . . the patient feels that the container for his feelings has been destroyed, and therefore has himself to build up a very strong container. He needs a kind of wall or castle in order to keep the pressure from getting out of control.
>
> *Rosenfeld (1987, p. 215)*

The concept of failure

With narcissistic patients there is a constant demand for provision of one sort or another. Balint has contained this idea of the different sorts of demands that can be made of the analyst in his concepts of 'benign' regression which desires 'recognition' and 'malignant' regression which demands 'gratification'. Analysts fear that this demand from the patient is going to be insatiable and that they will be seduced/manipulated into responding sexually or with retaliatory aggression.

With these patients failure can come from any source – either from the analyst's fear of his or her own sexual or aggressive response or from the patient's need to demand from and attack the holding containment of the analytic provision. According to Sechehaye (1951), once the patient's deep need has been understood, there is no question of insatiability. Going along with this framework a patient would be seen as needy and not greedy. Nevertheless, failure is all too easy if we do not manage to reach the patient through the narrow range of his possibilities.

Conclusion

In treating this kind of patient by ordinary analysis one learns an enormous amount about narcissism, but how far do we actually succeed in helping them (Pierce Clark, 1933)? The old question does not seem to have changed much. An increasing number of theorists, including Balint and Winnicott, Bion (1962), and Nissim Momigliano and Robutti (1992), all propose that a patient of this sort gains more through emotional experience that is shared, than merely through interpretations from the analyst which could become persecutory. Shared experience includes the mirroring experience where the demand for a certain symmetry in the analyst–patient relationship is respected without the analyst losing his or her boundaries or letting the sharing deteriorate into a *folie-à-deux*. In this sense Resnik's (1995) concept of 'double transference' rather than transference and countertransference is pertinent.

In any event the prognosis of these patients is poor. If it does come, change comes about very slowly. Freud (1914) was not wrong when he claimed that their resistance was 'unconquerable'. Whether they clamour for insight or not, the 'how', 'what' and 'why' is rarely understood by them (Bion, 1967) given that the idealised primary object is untouchable. The analyst may invest a lot of energy over a long period of time, but he or she has to be prepared for the fact that it may well turn out to be an analysis that goes nowhere as a result of the patient's early childhood experience of non-containment. The desire for change is frequently put into the analyst who can feel a lot of irritation and guilt, whereas the patient him- or herself periodically accepts grains of truth.

However, it is imperative not to lose sight of these patients' search for connection, even through their destructive attacks, because we must remember that, however vicious their behaviour, they are trying to re-experience the missing connectedness of their primary attachment. If the analyst does lose sight of the narcissist's urgent desire for connection, he or she (the analyst) may well experience a more intensive onslaught of attacks.

Thus the idea of the search for connectedness may give us a more relevant lead into the treatment than one of regression. It is not our idea to underestimate the importance of regression in the treatment of this sort of patient. Regression may signal either a hope of 'recognition' or a compulsive drive towards 'gratification' (Balint, 1968; Khan, 1969). For example, with the same patient whom we have previously mentioned, when there is any hint of separateness between us (i.e. a need for clarification or a disagreement), the patient shows the most extreme distress and aggression. I insist on relating his rage to his disbelief that we can be separate and both survive: connected without being merged.

However, underlying any sort of regression is the unconscious notion of primitive contact. This is phantasised as either broken or sustained. The analyst should always be aware that, in the repetition of earlier 'smashings', the patient is trying to find the original unbroken contact with his primary object (Little, 1985).

Summary

To summarise the relevant points:

- The narcissistic transference is different from the ordinary transference neurosis because it involves the revival of archaic objects rather than the instinctual investment of Oedipal conflicts.
- These patients are trying to re-experience the missing connectedness of their primary attachment.
- The experience that they lack and the one that they are longing to

find is one that we define as *the right degree of connectedness*.

- Once these patients' deep need has been understood (although we all know this is no easy matter), there is no question of insatiability. Going along with this framework a patient would be seen as needy and not greedy.
- This feeling of connectedness, when re-established, enables the patient to have both a good internal object and a good external reference point.
- In the repetition of earlier 'smashings', the patient is trying to find the original unbroken contact. Therefore, the importance for the analyst/therapist with this type of patient is to keep the treatment going in spite of the exhaustion and projected hopelessness involved.

References

Balint M (1968). *The Basic Fault: Therapeutic Aspects of Regression*. London: Tavistock.

Bion WR (1962). *Learning from Experience*. London: Heinemann. Reprinted in 1984 by Karnac Books, London.

Bion WR (1967). *Second Thoughts*. London: Heinemann. Reprinted in 1987 by Karnac Books, London.

Bollas C (1979). The transformational object. *International Journal of Psycho-Analysis* 60: 97–107.

Bowlby J (1971). *Attachment and Loss*, vol. 1, *Attachment*. London: Hogarth Press.

Fairbairn WRD (1956). A critical evaluation of certain basic psycho-analytical conceptions. *British Journal of Philosophical Science* 7: 49–60.

Freud A (1954). Psycho-analysis and education. *Psychoanalytic Study of the Child* 9: 9–15.

Freud A (1976). As quoted by AS Couch (1987) in an unpublished paper 'Anna Freud's adult psychoanalytic technique'.

Freud S (1909). Notes upon a case of obsessional neurosis. *The Complete Psychological Works of Sigmund Freud*, standard edition, vol. 10. London: Hogarth Press.

Freud S (1914). On narcissism: an introduction. *The Complete Psychological Works of Sigmund Freud*, standard edition, vol.14. London: Hogarth Press.

Glasser M (1992). Problems in the psychoanalysis of certain narcissistic disorders. *International Journal of Psycho-Analysis* 73: 493–503.

Grunberger B (1989). *New Essays on Narcissism*. London: Free Association Books.

Kernberg O (1977). *Borderline Conditions and Pathological Narcissism*. New York: Jason Aronson.

Khan MMR (1963). The concept of cumulative trauma. In: *The Privacy of the Self*. London: Hogarth Press, 1974.

Khan MMR (1969). An essay on Balint's researches on the theory of psycho-analytic technique. *International Journal of Psycho-Analysis* 50: 237–48.

Kohut H (1971). *The Analysis of the Self*. London: Hogarth Press.

Little MI (1985). Winnicott working in areas where psychotic anxieties predominate. *Free Associations* 3: 9–42.

Lomas P (1987). *The Limits of Interpretation*. Harmondsworth: Penguin.

Nissim Momigliano L, Robutti A (1992). *Shared Experience*. London: Karnac Books.

Pierce Clark L (1933). The question of prognosis in narcissistic neuroses and psychoses. *International Journal of Psycho-Analysis* 14: 71–86.

Resnik S (1995). *Mental Space*. London: Karnac Books.

Rosenfeld H (1965). *Psychotic States*. London: Hogarth Press.

Rosenfeld H (1987). *Impasse and Interpretation*. London: Routledge.

Sechehaye MA (1951). *Symbolic Realization*. New York: International Universities Press.

Steiner J (1993). *Psychic Retreats*. London, New York: Routledge.

Winnicott DWW (1948). Paediatrics and psychiatry. In: *Collected Papers: Through Paediatrics to Psycho-Analysis*. London: Tavistock, 1958.

Winnicott DWW (1953). Transitional objects and transitional phenomena. In: *Collected Papers: Through Paediatrics to Psycho-Analysis*. London: Tavistock, 1958.

Winnicott DWW (1958). *Collected Papers: Through Paediatrics to Psycho-Analysis*. London: Tavistock.

Winnicott DWW (1971). *Playing and Reality*. London: Tavistock.

Chapter 11
'I am glad I am late'

DANIEL TWOMEY

This chapter deals with the narcissistic structure of a patient as the main focus of his treatment.

Mr P arrives for his session 35 minutes late. Comes into the room. Doesn't respond to my saying 'Hello'. Takes off his jacket. Hangs it on the chair. Then checks that it is straight and without wrinkles. Puts his keys and wallet on to the couch. Sits on the couch. Takes off his shoes. Then lies on the couch. Makes some grunting, stretching, yawning noises. Eventually finds a comfortable place. Turns on his side, and goes to sleep. Three minutes before the end of the session, I say 'It's nearly time'. He wakes up. Then puts his shoes on, checks his wallet and keys, puts them in the pocket of his jacket, and leaves. He does not say 'Goodbye'.

In the next session, Mr P arrives 30 minutes late. He goes through exactly the same ritual on entering as in the first session, lying on the couch, and saying: 'I'm upset. People at work have upset me. I came into work this morning; no-one said hello to me; I noticed everybody else was talking to each other.' I respond (being aware that I was irritated with him), saying 'I think yesterday you let me know very clearly why you have difficulties with colleagues at work, and in making friends. You came to the session yesterday; you didn't greet me, or respond to my greeting; you turned your back on me; fell asleep; and ignored me as if I wasn't there. Perhaps your colleagues at work treat you as they do because of the way you treat them.' He gets angry and explains that with me it is very different; that he can do as he likes when he is with me; that he's paying me; while at work it is totally different; and that (as usual) I'm talking nonsense. I find it very difficult to restrain myself from getting into an argument with Mr P, as one of the characteristics of working with him is his continuous attempts to engage me in debate.

In describing these two sessions I hope to enable the reader to sense the tone and quality of our communications. His continuous ignoring of me, treating me as if I did not exist, except as an object or an extension of himself, to be used, manipulated and discarded at will, proved difficult.

Mr P came into therapy as he was finding it impossible to make friends or form relationships. At our first meeting he set, very clearly, the tone of our future interactions. He was mistrustful, demanding to be told what to do about his life. At the end of our first meeting, when we discussed fees, I explained to him that he would be responsible for missed sessions, and I would expect him to take his holidays at the same time as myself; he objected strenuously, and said that before he made up his mind to come into treatment with me he would have to do some research. He left, looking grumpy and suspicious, while I wondered whether I really wanted to take him into treatment.

At the next session, Mr P said that he reluctantly accepted my terms because he had done some research. He knew people who were in therapy and he had telephoned them all and asked them how their therapists behaved in respect of missed sessions and holidays. They all told him that their therapists behaved as I had proposed. So he decided he would try, but insisted that he did not like it and that he was not happy with the terms, and hoped that at a future date I would become more reasonable, and be prepared to re-negotiate them with him.

Throughout his treatment, lateness was a continual characteristic, and for a long time he was not amenable to interpretation. He told me, several times, that he was pleased to come late because then he felt in control. When I spoke about the aggressive component of this he pointed out that he was paying me and it did not matter, I was his servant; he said this with great delight and triumph. At other times, he told me he came late because he was afraid that he would have nothing to say or that he would fall asleep. Fear and terror of closeness were discussed and related to me in the transference, to his friends and colleagues, and to his family. This did not seem to change his timekeeping. However, interpretations about his aggressiveness eventually enabled him to attend more punctually.

Throughout the sessions, sleep was another main characteristic of his means of communicating with me. Very early in the treatment, in mid-sentence, he would fall asleep. Sometimes he seemed, from eye movements and quivers, to be dreaming. But seldom did he report a dream when he woke up. Falling asleep began to irritate him and he decided he would sit on a chair, to see if that would keep him awake. However, this proved unsuccessful and still, in the middle of sentences, he would slump forward and fall asleep. In the early days of treatment I found myself responding in a relaxed, thoughtful way to his sleeping, and wondered if perhaps he was re-living times when he had felt safe with a parent.

> The earliest memory that can appear in the analytic situation is sleep on the couch. It repeats the nursing situation and a wish for narcissistic sleep.
>
> *Lewin (1954)*

However, as time went on, I began to observe that, often, during his sleeping time, I felt irritated, and began to see his sleeping as defensive as well as a re-enactment and an expression of his hostility.

> Falling asleep is a subtle form of hostility manifested by omnipotent intrusion into one's object.
>
> *Alexander (1976)*

He was in treatment for 2–3 years before being able to recall that his mother had been a very distressed and erratic woman; she was frequently irrationally angry; she was extremely jealous of her children's relationship with their father, and listened in to their telephone conversations. She objected strongly to the visits of family relatives, who were warm and affectionate, and of whom he has many happy memories — for instance, playing pillow fights with them – until his mother's jealousy made it impossible.

Now, Mr P's sleeping, I felt, had changed in its communication to me, from his initial need to be in a secure place safe with an adult watching, to the avoidance of the attentions of a very intrusive and distressed parent.

His distrust of me was enormous throughout his treatment. At times, for good reasons, he had to cancel a session and I was able to offer him an alternative time. However, the fact that this happened never lessened his complaints about my charging for missed sessions and his vision of me as a greedy person. On accepting an interpretation referring to his past, he would often return the next day looking triumphant and angry. He would have discussed what I had said in detail with his father, who would then have produced photographic evidence proving that what I had said was total nonsense and was certainly not applicable to him. My only reason for saying these things was to keep him in treatment, to make me rich. Often such patients unconsciously realise the paucity of what they offer and that money is the only thing of value and importance that they can give, and which they can feel, in a grandiose way, keeps the therapist going.

At one stage during the treatment, I felt that there was something very strange and peculiar happening. I did not understand the language of his communications, as it seemed to have changed. Eventually, I decided to share with him this uneasy, inexplicable feeling in the session. To my surprise, and slight shock, he told me that he had been seeing another therapist as well as me, but he had not wanted me to know this. When I made the comment 'Well, we have to think about what to do about this', he became angry, told me it was none of my business and that he could see whomever he liked. When I insisted that we would have to think about it, he very cleverly told me that I was like his mother who objected to his relationship with his family relatives.

Secretiveness is a very strong characteristic of Mr P. I began to understand it in terms of his fear that his mother/I would destroy anything good that he had found. He had found a girlfriend and had been seeing her for some time, and only when he decided that she was not suitable for him was he able to tell me about it. He explained to me that he felt that, if he had told me about her when he first met her, he would no longer have been free to explore the relationship; he would have been subject to my influence and I might have said something that would have totally destroyed it. He had similar attitudes – to taking up hobbies, such as attending a gymnasium, or dieting – which I must not be told about. I interpreted this as his desire to protect for himself something good from the destructive, jealous mother/me who would not allow him to explore his relationships outside the home in a private way; but that he would feel under pressure to fulfil my/the mother's wishes for him.

He found it, as is obvious enough from the above, very difficult to free associate. At times he told me that he could imagine himself losing bowel and bladder control, and that would be more acceptable than to tell me what was going on in his mind.

Not surprisingly, as with so many narcissistic patients, he found it almost impossible to symbolise. For instance, at one session he adopted the expression that he wanted to let his anger out. This became concretised by him – it was experienced as real – as having some horrible bad liquid inside him that needed to be let out. Attempts to interpret this in terms of bad objects inside him proved futile. Eventually, after many weeks of work, he accepted that it was a metaphor or a symbol for his hate and envy towards me/the mother on whom he wished 'to let it out'. The move from concreteness to metaphor and symbolism was quite an achievement.

He found it impossible to accept me as separate from himself. He talked about '*We* must do this . . .'. For instance, sometimes, having spoken to me for a few minutes, he would suddenly say 'What shall we do now, as I don't want to go to sleep'. The idea of the 'we' being composed of two separate 'I's was very difficult for him, if not impossible. For instance, he argued that because he told me what was in his mind then I should tell him what was in my mind. The idea that the mother-and-child or the patient-and-therapist can have separate roles, separate functions, was unbearable. He was very stuck with the idea of being merged with me. In that way he could control me to be there for him and only him when he wanted me.

He did not acknowledge any need of me or what I could offer him; his continuous wish to annoy me and to resist insight was expressed by attempts to engage me in didactic argumentative debates. For instance, the idea that his depression and illness when saying goodbye to family and friends might be connected to earlier separations was argued against strenuously. His father was quoted as a witness that he had never been deprived, separated or rejected. He clung tenaciously to the equation: 'If it never happened concretely, I can never or will never feel it.'

Narcissism is deeply antagonistic to self-knowledge.

Symington (1993)

It was very striking how his father and I were played off against one another. Once or twice he smilingly told me that he did not tell his father everything I said – only the things that he knew would give his father ammunition for arguing with and contradicting me. His need to recreate a warring parental couple vying for his affection was clear.

His helplessness was mostly covered over by an omnipotence that made him think of himself as unique: 'not like other helpless fellow mortals.' He told me that at 12 he decided he would opt out of 'being one of the group', and would lead his own life in his own way. This, for the first 5 years of therapy, was something that he was extremely proud of, and, after many discussions and interpretations, he began to accept that, yes, the price of uniqueness was also total loneliness and isolation. This isolation at times bordered on annihilation: no friends, no colleagues – never meeting anybody at weekends – just being on his own. He bought a flat, and it was more than 3 years before he was able to have a cooker installed, although he had been given one as a present. At first, this was omnipotently boasted about – he didn't need a cooker, he didn't need people. A house-warming present of a television set was given the same treatment – being left in the box. The flat was never, for those years, seen as anything other than as a place where he could be the oddball and the outsider. However, it was noticeable, after further time in treatment, that the cooker was installed. And curtains were bought. Friends were invited to the flat, to share a meal.

The interpretative work that led to the flat beginning to be a home came after we had both started to see that he was identifying totally with the mother of his childhood, who never allowed visitors, or friends, to come to the family home, which she complained was never finished or ready. When he realised how strong this identification was, he became extremely anxious and worried. And then told me that one of the greatest fears he had had in his life was that he might become like his mother.

Mr P is the second child in a family of four children. He was convinced that in primary school he was very happy. He had home movies of school journeys as evidence to prove this, although he could remember his mother's jealousy of his relatives being a problem. Otherwise, he saw his early life as idyllic, that is, until the penultimate year of his junior school, when he reached puberty at 9 years and, because of his academic brilliance, was moved up a class higher than his age group. From then on, he felt everything had gone wrong. At 12, he remembers, as mentioned above, making the conscious decision to become the oddball, to do the opposite of what everybody else did – which meant no participation in group activities or having any close friends. However, he got to university, and read for a degree in fine arts. He did not make friends, and on finishing university he went into education.

When he had his first nocturnal emission he was confused and puzzled, because he had no idea what it was. However, his mother noticed it, and said, rather sadly 'Oh, my boy', which he heard as something that his mother felt deeply regretful and critical about. He did not discover masturbation until he was 23 and, at 27, he had his first sexual experience with a woman, which still lived on in his mind as something very important and good. After that, as far as I knew, his only sexual experience had been with prostitutes. He continuously craved affection, and went searching, in pubs, anywhere, hoping to find a partner. He could readily accept and acknowledge that his wishes and phantasies of being with a partner were very much those of a child-being-with-his-mother. They very rarely contained sexual phantasies, but were about being held, being close and being warm. He slept every night with a teddy-bear. Longing for his mother was expressed by falling asleep, outside his flat in the car, listening to gentle music. Longing to be dependent was intense, but when it became revived in the transference he shrunk away aggressively. Through his masturbation phantasies, he imagined being both male and female, confirming his omnipotent self-sufficiency.

> The libido that has been withdrawn from the external world has been directed to the ego and thus gives rise to an attitude which may be called narcissism.
>
> *Freud (1914)*

Another aspect of Mr P's psyche was an excessive inhibition about speaking to people. Often he could go for days torturing himself about his need to ask a question of a colleague or friend. Often I experienced enormous pressure to give him a formula of words to use for making a simple request. He had phantasies of being attacked or abused if he made a simple demand. It was as if his wishes to be masochistically passive were frightening and terrifying. Gradually this symptom decreased, as a result of interpretation about his passive, masochistic needs as they appeared in the transference, particularly his demands that I wake him up or prevent him from falling asleep.

> The patient chose this particular form of resistance (falling asleep) because, by it, he could also give expression to unconscious passive homoerotic phantasies – a phantasy of being overpowered during sleep
>
> *(Ferenczi, 1914).*

Mr P's hatred and envy, of other people being separate and different from him, was intense. If, in a depressed mood, he observed happy people in the street, he wanted to shoot them down, with a machine-gun. He found it extremely difficult to accept any interpretation that he had not already had some notion of in his own thoughts. He seemed to be saying: 'How dare you have a thought that's different from mine, because when you do then you're separate, not merged with me!' On these occasions it was necessary for me to be very still and not to persist with the interpretations, but rather to acknowledge his anger with me.

I will now give some snippets of sessions when we were working on termination, in the hope that it will give the reader some idea of the changes that had occurred in Mr P since the beginning of treatment 9 years before.

On one occasion, he arrived 10 minutes late, looking tired, and complained about the cushions at the side of the couch. He said he would like to ask me more about them, but he did not think he would 'waste his time' as I would not answer him. (I noted that he did not seem to have any wish to argue, or to debate, and was acknowledging our separateness.)

He had achieved a big success at work, was feeling proud of himself and wished he could celebrate his good fortune; on noticing two colleagues happily engaged in conversation he suddenly felt a blushing, burning sensation on his left cheek and wished he could speak to me – or someone else – because he was frightened of being unable to control his blushing. My interpretation was that his awareness of the need for me and others to celebrate his success had caused him to blush with embarrassment lest I and his colleagues should know his great secret, namely that he had a need for others. He then told me that on the previous evening he had left his father's house earlier than he had intended, as his father was getting too excited celebrating some good news of his own.

On one occasion, he arrived for a session 'only 15 minutes late', having almost forgotten to come. He said he was glad he had forgotten, because 'that means that I am freer'. I interpreted that perhaps he felt freer, and able to forget, now that we had decided to finish therapy at the end of the month. He laughed mockingly, and said: 'How funny, so the best thing I've ever done since I met you is to leave. How very funny!' I was aware of feeling irritated at the way he had turned my interpretation upside-down, which indeed had happened many times throughout the therapy. I commented that only now he was leaving could he acknowledge some freedom. If he were not leaving, freedom might be dangerous: it might trigger off some intimate feelings towards me which might make it more difficult to leave. He responded in a rather didactic, lecturing, way: 'I'd better inform you that I won't miss you. You are not a person. You are only someone I came to see to talk about my problems.'

> The core of narcissism is a hatred of the relational – a hatred of something that is inherent in our being.
>
> *Symington (1993)*

'I might be sad if I heard you had died.' I commented that it seems that I had to die before he could miss me. And then it would not be a shared feeling between us.

He had found somebody at work with whom he shared an interest, and this has pleased him a lot, the interest being *all methods of transport*. But he was worried that people would think that he was odd. He said 'Calling someone a train spotter is really derogatory'. I commented that he experienced me as a robot-like thing that he used to tell his problems to. I was an object, not a person. I said perhaps the train spotter in him was worried lest people think him more interested in machines than people. That perhaps he felt that he had been derogatory towards me, treating me as a 'train', to be spotted and then to be ignored and forgotten until the train was cast off in death.

He had begun to think about buying a flat nearer central London, which I had commented on as perhaps being a way of moving closer to me. Then he began to talk about some people at work who had left the Company, and remembered a saying: 'You only miss people/things when you've either lost them or they're gone.' I felt that this was pretty obviously what would happen: that I could only be missed when I was gone, and couldn't be missed when I was available. Rather than interpret these remarks in relation to me, I said: 'Perhaps you feel that about your mother since her death: that you miss her more now that she is gone.' He said: 'I think you might also be thinking that I might feel that about you in the future.'

He told me how he tended to cry during films in which there were funeral scenes and men were being mocked. He identified strongly with a character who behaved like an idiot and eventually became successful. I interpreted to him that his tears were safe in the cinema and that also he was letting me know that, even though he might be presenting himself, at times, like the character in the film, there was a belief within him that he would be successful, and that perhaps after he had finished therapy this might come about. I thought, but did not say, that perhaps for him the only way that he could allow the therapy to be of benefit to him was when it was finished.

> The analysis could not begin to 'take' until after she had lived through the psychic experience of being born. She felt she could not be born except by leaving analysis.
>
> *Milner (1949)*

In the penultimate week, he wondered whether to use the couch or the chair, saying that to experience a full session on the couch was somewhat akin to dying, likening it to a fire that would not light: 'I'm here, lying here, waiting for you to say something. I imagine you're waiting for me to say something. So the fire doesn't get lit by you or by me. And that I'm hoping you will light the fire, and maybe you are hoping that I will light it.' I commented that I thought that for the first time he had let me know how lonely he had felt on the couch in his silences, and that perhaps that was one of the reasons why he slept so much – to avoid the sense of my not being there to help him to light the fire within him, or of not being able to do it himself. He said: 'I feel better, but still have a lot of problems.' I said that I felt that he was telling me that I must be careful not to get any ideas that therapy was any good to him – he was letting me know that he still had his problems, although he might be feeling better and freer. He said: 'Well, I'm totally agnostic on this. I am certainly much better, more at ease with myself than when I first came into therapy. But I have no idea how much of that is attributable to therapy, or how much of it is just something that would have happened anyway!' I commented that he again felt that he must be very careful, because if therapy had been any use to him it might make it more difficult for him to say good-bye. Again he responded, saying he was not going to miss me, and that he did not want to hear 'any more of this kind of talk'; if he had problems he could talk to his father, brothers, sister; and anyway, the Samaritans were always available.

Then he spoke about how he would be more ordinary when he had left. I commented that I represented a mad mother for him, and that he couldn't feel sane or ordinary until he had got away from me/the mad mother.

> It was only after the patient felt that I had been bad to her by 'chucking her out' that she had been able to recognise her hate of her mother and so become free enough to begin life as a separate person.
>
> *Milner (1949)*

Then he told me that he had had a thought that I might tell him that I was leaving him my paintings. I commented that this sounded quite an affectionate thought: it was seeing me as a father who was leaving my son-and-heir my paintings, which would be of interest to him, as an artist. I was aware, but did not say it, that there was also a death wish contained in that thought.

In his last session he brought a dream which contained most of the main subjects we had worked on throughout the therapy. On waking up, his first thought had been 'Oh, after today, I won't have Daniel to tell my dreams to'. I noted that this was the first real acknowledgement that he was going to miss me. He asked 'If I wrote to you and told you a dream like that would you post me back an interpretation?'. I felt it was important to answer that question directly, and I said 'No'. Then he said: 'Ah, so, I have no safety-net. I would like to have some safety-net, even the little safety-net of a letter. But now it feels that's taken away.' He looked extremely sad and vulnerable. He said he couldn't think of any possible reason for writing to me if he didn't have a problem to tell me. I felt that he had touched on missing me personally, and had now gone back to seeing me as more of a computer man who would just sort out his problems. He said there wouldn't be any point, would there, in telling you: 'Oh, I'm very happy, I've got a new flat. I've got a wife and I'm happy. Or, unfortunately my father died and I am very sad. What would you say? What would be the point of writing that kind of a letter to you if you wouldn't answer and give me some interpretation about it?' I said that I felt that he was struggling very hard at acknowledging that he was going to miss me. But he said 'I suppose if I did want I could come back and see you, just for one session'. I agreed that this was possible. But he still felt very disappointed that he was unable to get psychotherapy at a distance, by post. He worried that maybe he would never change, i.e. by having a wife and family; but, on the other hand, he was aware now that being single had advantages, e.g. freedom and not being responsible to anybody. However, he did express his concern about being alone. I commented that he was becoming free of me but worried about losing his attachment to me. He said he had been very worried and frightened about what would happen if he became involved with a woman and she had 10 friends and he had no friend except her; then he would become unbearable in his demands. He then said he would be equally frightened if he had friends and his future wife didn't have any. She would be very dependent on him. And he would lose all his freedom. I commented about the old fear of either being isolated, with no friends, or being suffocated by too many. He would suffocate or be suffocated.

He left, feeling rather sad. I wished him well and was left wondering whether I should have been warmer, and given him some concrete reminder of therapy, e.g. a book, or something. But I thought that this would be far too dangerous, because it might have been interpreted as the act of a clinging mother wanting to keep him under her control, by providing a constant reminder of her presence.

References

Alexander RP (1976). On patients who sleep during the psychoanalytic session. *Contemporary Psychoanalysis* **12**(3).

Ferenczi S (1914). On falling asleep during analysis. In: *Further Contributions to the Theory and Technique of Psycho-Analysis*. London: Hogarth Press.

Freud S (1914). On narcissism. *The Complete Psychological Works of Sigmund Freud*, standard edition, vol. 14. London: Hogarth Press.

Lewin BD (1954). Sleep, narcissistic neurosis, and the psychoanalytic situation. *Psychoanalytic Quarterly* **23**: 487–509.

Milner M (1949). On finishing analysis. In: *The Suppressed Madness of Sane Men*. London: Routledge.

Symington N (1993). *Narcissism. A New Theory*. London: Karnac Books.

Chapter 12
Destroying the knowledge of the need for love: narcissism and perversions

DAVID MORGAN

Since Freud originally wrote about perversions in the 'Three essays' (1905) the primary focus for this difficult area has moved from the Oedipal scenario to a pre-Oedipal one. A perversion can now be seen as a defence against a number of difficulties not necessarily related to a regression from the Oedipal conflict, but much more to the result of difficulties in the early years of life. It always takes as its object something representing the primary object, the mother. In this sense it is a defence against psychosis, an attempt to deal with destructiveness towards the object, which could lead to breakdown and disintegration. It is narcissistic in that the damaged or absent maternal object is replaced by a phantasy object that is felt to be entirely under the control of the subject.

For example, a patient's memory of childhood was the rubber mattress that he used to turn to as a baby in his cot when he felt abandoned by his mother. This can be seen as defensive, in that his destructive feelings towards her were so great that he destroyed his knowledge of anything that she could provide him with and gave it to something over which he felt he had some control. Later, after he was married, this became a full rubber fetish and he would climb inside a rubber suit which would provide him with soothing comfort in any crisis. This auto-erotic substitute with which to cope with anxiety at the same time forced his wife, who was described as frigid, into a subservient position *vis-à-vis* his sexual activity, putting her into the role of a voyeur. Thus he eliminated his own feelings of helplessness by sexualising a dead inanimate object, which was felt to be totally under his power, at the same time destroying any knowledge of his need for love by stripping his collusive wife of any comfort that she could offer him, putting her in the place of the redundant primary object, projecting the unwanted bad feelings into her, while he retained all the feelings of potency through owning the source of his gratification. Thus, in the perversions, aggression and anxiety caused by early fears of disintegration become eroticised and powerful rather than disintegrating into a terrifying descent into psychosis.

If a part of one's own body becomes fetishised in this way, or some material such as rubber or leather closely resembling the skin, or clothing such as that used in transvestism, the accompanying unconscious phantasy is that the source of gratification is in the pursuit of this object. Other people are often involved but they play a secondary role which is very circumscribed and controlled. They become an 'accomplice' (Khan, 1979). For instance a transvestite is often married but, like the TV personality Edna Everidge and her stooge Madge, the real woman is turned into the impoverished object which is triumphed over. I have been impressed at how many partners of male transvestites have undergone early hysterectomies – the result of the destructive envious assaults on their real female qualities.

Heimann (1952) states:

> . . . the essential difference between infantile and mature object relations is that, whereas the adult conceives of the object as existing independently of himself, for the infant it always refers in some way to itself.

This description of object-relations encompasses introjection in which objects become identified with a part of themselves; thus the infant sucks his thumb and feels himself to be in contact with the breast. This creates phantasies of having incorporated the breast and a feeling that he can produce his own gratification. Thus pathological narcissism is a state of autoerotic gratification. In the perversions, we can often see that the form of the activity indulged in often contains a very accurate communication of the original breakdown or problem. They are by their very nature activities that precede symbolic functioning and therefore contain concrete forms of mental problems. This is the reason that narcissistic patients have great difficulty in symbolising. For example, a woman, who had been sexually abused by her own father for several years while a pre-pubescent child, felt driven to setting fires in her 8-year-old daughter's bedroom. In this way she projected the inflamed part of herself into an object, attempting to gain control over her own disturbing experience by projecting it entirely into the other, in this case her daughter, someone who most closely resembled herself at the age it happened.

Pathological narcissism as manifested in the perversions occurs where the need to have absolute control over the object has been so great that the equivalent phantasy of the thumb, the rubber fetish, for instance, becomes idealised. The pervert has identified a part of the self, or invested an action or behaviour as the good object, i.e. the transvestite in phantasy becomes the mother and the bad parts are projected outside into the external objects. Getting into the object, dressing up as a woman or as in the case of a transsexual 'becoming a woman' takes over all the primary object's qualities, enviously taking all the good so that the patient/infant becomes the source of gratification; any other object being the source of it has to be robbed and devalued as with the transvestite's wife or the arsonist's 8-year-old daughter. The victim is subjugated and forced to carry the unwanted aspects of the self.

There is enormous hostility against any awareness that life and goodness lie outside the self. Destructiveness therefore dominates, particularly in those whose early experience has been traumatic and impoverished. If a narcissistic patient was to become aware of his envy towards the object it would be tantamount to acknowledging that it was the source of gratification and was not a part of himself. This would be unbearable and the acknowledgement of separateness and dependency has to be defended against at all cost. In extreme pathological narcissism, as in the perversions, this knowledge has to be entirely avoided. This can mean absolute destruction of the other as an entity except as an object to have control over. Cruelty and hate have to dominate, e.g. a man who indulged in cottaging and cruising (that is, promiscuous homosexual sex in lavatories and public places), after 5 years of analysis, came to feel that something he was getting from me was useful. There had been considerable diminishment of his perversion to the point where he no longer felt the need to find violent 'rough trade' strangers with whom to be intimate. He was able to work without getting into fights and was developing a number of long-term friends whom he valued. Consequently his wish to deal with his destructive feelings through masochism intensified in the transference. After a weekend he came back to his Monday session and discovered to his 'surprise' that the chairs usually in the waiting area were not there. He took this to mean that I did not care about him anymore, so although it was raining heavily outside he decided to sit on the doorstep. I was surprised to discover that he was not in my new waiting room some few feet away from where the old waiting area had been. It was not until some time after I had found him on the step that he disclosed to me his reason for sitting outside.

We discovered that he had forgotten that I had told him I was making a change to my waiting area; he acknowledged that he had known and we were able to explore his reasons for forgetting. He angrily acknowledged his wish to set me up as a cruel uncaring analyst. His growing awareness of his need for me had led him to set things up so that I could be seen as entirely uncaring; his trust in me could then be proved to be unfounded and he could return to the inhuman environments he had previously frequented. At least he did not have expectations of any humanity there and would not be conned by unscrupulous analysts. This need to maintain a cruel and narrow-minded environment has been described by Brenman (1985) and Sohn (1985).

In severe forms of perversion, such as paedophilia or sexual murder, the need to destroy completely any goodness in the other is all powerful. For instance, a paedophile remembered his own abuse; while at a children's home he ran away to London at the age of 12 and was picked up by a man who, under the pretext of caring for him, brutally buggered him and abandoned him. He could remember these awful experiences with all the attendant pain and anger, but was unable in any way to associate his own abuse with the violent sexual abuse of his 12-year-old victims whom he would trap in a block of council flats. Thus he dealt with the memory of his own experience by negating the experience of the other. The other became merely a way of ridding himself of what was painful and bad for him, which could be sadistically and physically put into the victim. He would describe how aggrieved he was with his victims when enacting this abuse, while at the same time, in another part of the session, feeling tearful at the reminder of his own abandonment at the hands of his erstwhile saviour who had abused him.

As Bollas (Edward Glover Lecture, 1993) has pointed out, those who have had to annihilate large parts of themselves to survive can only feel alive when they are annihilating the other. The serial killer will describe in detail the sense of relief and pleasure at having total power over his victim because, at that moment all the badness, the impoverishment is in the victim and not in himself. It is he who is in a position to annihilate other selves which gives him relief through the projection of his own psychic state into the other. It is this defence against the death instinct, which has primary envy at its source, that lies at the heart of all perverse activity.

This denial of the other as being the source of love and comfort leads the patient to act destructively. This destructiveness is a defence against the knowledge of the need for love. The more this knowledge has to be destroyed, the more the other has to be enslaved, marginalised and, in the final scenario, killed. The act of total destruction only occurs in extreme circumstances as the need for an object into whom to project the unwanted parts necessitates its survival. However, in the serial abuser or killer this has been circumvented.

As one object dies another can be used to replace it. This of course again reflects their own experience of negligence at the hands of others.
Rosenfeld (1971) states:

> . . . that in consideration of narcissism from the libidinal aspect one can see that the over evaluation of the self plays a central role based on idealisation of the self. Self idealisation is maintained by omnipotent introjective and projective identifications with good objects and their qualities.

In this way the narcissist experiences all objects as part of himself or as omnipotently controlled by himself.

In the pervert, failure in the environment has been so great that there is a need to withdraw all sources of gratification from the external world and to give them to a part of the self.

Skirting around the issue: pathological narcissism and transsexualism

Christy Brown (1990) describes transsexualism as a profound disturbance of psychological gender development from well before puberty, with both the subjective sense of gender (gender identity) and gender-specific behaviour (gender-role behaviour) being discordant with manifest anatomical gender. Feminine interests are strikingly displayed. There is intense dislike of the genitalia and, from puberty, of the secondary sexual characteristics. Sexual orientation is homosexual, towards others of the same anatomical sex, but this is sometimes seen by the patient as heterosexuality on a subjective level because his phantasies are of being a woman in sexual activity with men. Behaviours that develop are aimed at increasing the expression of the gender disorder; these commonly include cross-dressing, the wearing of women's clothes, but with a sense of comfort rather than sexual arousal. There is a painful search for help and usually for medical and surgical treatment aimed at reassignment as a woman. The level of interest in sexual activity is low.

This general description of transsexualism is confirmed by Limentani (1979) who states that most workers in the field would regard the following as transsexual: any child, adolescent or adult who expresses a claim to be trapped in the wrong biological body; where there is evidence of a complete dislike or appreciation of primary and secondary characteristics of the appropriate sex, often accompanied by a compelling and urgent desire for hormone treatment and plastic surgery.

The aetiology of transsexualism is, however, uncertain. Brown (1990) describes it as probably the result of a disorder or derailment of personality development rather than a disease. In spite of this, the major treatment is now more than ever oriented towards medical and surgical 'reassignment' by surgeons specialising in castration, mastectomy and the artificial creation of sexual organs. The results of this intervention are difficult to assess because of the relatively poor outcome studies. The reported improvement rate of 70% is therefore open to question (Abramowitz, 1986).

The dangers of treating a developmental problem with physical treatment are demonstrated by a case seen at the Portman Clinic. A man with a background of suicidal ideation and sexual abuse by his mother was given a 'sex change operation' to become a woman. He was castrated and fitted with a plastic vagina which needed to be dilated to 'work' and had silicone implants for 'breasts'. He then 'went to work as a female prostitute'. After a few years he began to feel that he would like relationships with women again. He eventually began to feel that the surgeon had robbed him of the possibility of a heterosexual experience, although he admitted that he had himself lied about his background to facilitate a surgical treatment. Another case involved a woman who had surgery to become a man. She underwent a mastectomy and was given an artificial penis which never functioned properly. She was left feeling that she could not function phallically, was suicidal and depressed. Before surgery she had also felt suicidal and she related this to child sexual abuse at the hands of her father. She too had not mentioned these experiences at her diagnostic interview because she did not consider it relevant to her gender problem. Blanchard (1985) found that, to obtain surgical treatment, transsexuals often falsify their history, so it would not be a surprise to discover that patients presenting are often unconsciously and sometimes consciously avoiding more complex problems.

Limentani (1979) states that transsexuality is a personality and character disaster that cannot be corrected by mutilating operations which are often carried out in response to threats of suicide amounting to blackmail. He says that the transsexual, in an attempt to provide relief from his symptoms, involves others in the phantasy.

At the Portman Clinic patients are seen both preoperatively and postoperatively for possible assessment for psychoanalytic psychotherapy. As a result of this we are in the position of exploring the patient's mental state without the need for convincing proof for surgical intervention. Often a different picture emerges – that of a patient with profound narcissistic disturbances in the early years of life. This diverges from the view of Limentani (1979) who states that, in his view, these patients are not psychotic and as a result are quite aware of the bizarreness of their current life but would prefer not to have them explored. Brown (1990) agrees with this view that in spite of the fairly high rate of other usually minor psychiatric morbidity, trans-sexuals often appear to be psychologically and socially normal in all respects apart from their specific gender disturbance. The experience of patients at the Portman Clinic would suggest that we are, in fact, dealing with profound psychotic anxieties resulting from extremely early trauma such as child abuse or extreme violence in the early years of life; this is often gender specific and leads to a wish to disidentify from the offending gender.

In consideration of this, the patients' problems should be explored by means other than physical in case we will be colluding with patients' delusional beliefs that changing reality will change them. The pressure to alter thinking and collude with these patients, who often threaten suicide, is great. Yet, as with other forms of disturbance, physical treatment although at first appearing fashionable may be disproved later on. However, the case of the current fashion for surgical treatment is irreversible.

The following cases illustrate ongoing clinical work with some patients.

Mr D

In a first diagnostic interview with Mr D, there was an enormous pressure to collude with his view of reality. He was thin and effeminate looking, rather camp in manner, like a woman slightly older than his age – a sort of rag trade type. He was dressed as a man. In his letter to the Clinic he had signed himself ambiguously as Teri and had used a letter heading establishing that he was a director of an organisation that enabled professionals to deal with violence in their work. He came to the point in a straightforward way saying that he had come to terms with being a woman and had booked his appointment with the surgeon but wanted somewhere he could think about the important step that he was taking. He felt that the Gender Dysphoria Clinic was hooked on the idea that it was a straightforward gender question whereas he was aware that it could be that he was a woman in a man's body or it could be to do with a problem with masculine figures. He had read the books and knew of the theories, and probably knew already where I stood in relation to all this. I said that it felt as if he were saying he was aware of differing perspectives, that he was even aware of what I already thought. I wondered if this certainty might have something to do with the problem of what my agenda might be in relation to him.

He had thought that I might be a woman. He put this down to the problem he has with masculine figures in general. He told me he was an only child and his mother was wonderful, totally accepting of him as he was, and had even entertained and enjoyed going out with his homosexual partners. In photos he was always next to mother whereas male figures were always distant. I mentioned his father and how distant he seemed; he grimaced saying father had been a cruel despot who had beaten both him and his mother and turned to alcohol. He was now totally cut off and estranged from his father and good riddance to him. He gave an idyllic account of how nice life had been between his mother and himself since father had left.

He moved quickly to the present and his work. He said that he had his own counselling practice although he had not done a training as such; previous therapy had always encouraged him to come out as himself and he now combined what he had learned there with gender questions about gay and lesbian issues. It created a picture of a transsexual presiding over a world of equal opportunity where all things were equal and with himself as the great egalitarian. Anyone who challenged this was a fascist. I was the unremitting analytic dictator. He had already let me know that he thought Freud was a bit backward in relation to gender. I had a bizarre vision of a man leading a group on violence, gradually turning into a woman. He did not consider that this would present many difficulties.

I said that he seemed to have moved quite easily from talking about his absent father to his position as a counsellor dealing with gender issues and violence, both issues that he had told me he might be interested in exploring with me here. I wondered if this was a common experience, that of not having something and with little pain actually trying to become or own it, meaning that one way of dealing with his own confusion was somehow to become an expert in helping other people with theirs. He was coming to see me for possible help in thinking about these issues but was telling me how good he was at advising others.

He then explained to me, in quite a different tone, various ideas on gender identity. I was an idiot and he was the expert. He said that he was and had always been gay even though he had also had heterosexual experiences. However, he was very aware that he did not want to grow up to be an old man. I had obvious thoughts about his wish to disidentify with his father, wanting to castrate himself as a way of getting rid of his old man. He felt that he was getting old and would be 40 soon and it would be too late. I thought that it was as if he was talking about the fact that he would be unable to have children, but what he thought he would give birth to would be a new him or her. He agreed that he knew he couldn't be a real woman, but even if he was he wouldn't have children anyway.

Throughout this I was made out to be the tough psychoanalyst dressed up in my theories. It was I who was 'skirting around the issue'. I was told that penis's could be got rid of without much problem or remorse. There was a lot of confusion in the session surrounding his identity; it was consistently felt to shift and the goal posts were moved on many occasions. He was himself a therapist counsellor who was advising others on gender problems and violence. The basic message seemed to be: if I castrate myself that is alright, but if you do not accept this then you are attacking, violating and mutilating my reality. Thus he dealt with his own confusion by projecting it.

I said to him that he had come here at one level to be able to think about things, but that this did not provide the certainty that he could get from other approaches to his problem. He described his experience of his previous therapist who had become pregnant after seeing him for one year. He thought he had been robbed and began a course of electrolysis. He saw this as the beginning of his move to become a woman leading on to contacting the Gender Dysphoria Trust. I said in a way he was letting me know that he had felt robbed and this had led him to run to other means of trying to help himself. He agreed and said that he felt that the Gender Dysphoria Trust had accepted the whole phantasy about cutting off parts of the self. I said he had been talking about how robbed and confused he had felt and that he turned to electrolysis on his body to cope with these feelings. He was able, in the interview, to acknowledge that changing one's body was not necessarily a satisfactory way of changing one's mind or dealing with painful feelings.

The session was full of this type of thing. He told me that his phantasy of being with a man while masquerading as a woman was that the other person would not know. He had a male friend who was a 'female' prostitute and his male clients did not know; thus he projected his confusion unknowingly, if that is possible, into the unconscious of the other person, reversing the confusing messages of his mother that he feels he has had to contain through identification. The other man becomes an unconscious participant in a homosexual act. Thus he has all the knowledge and the infantile position of not having knowledge is taken up by the man who is relating to a woman who is in reality male. His own confusion as a child, left in a world with his mother, with father absent, is reversed. He becomes the mother, getting inside her body and taking over all the primary object qualities, giving them to himself, and then he is in a position to seduce men. By enacting the seductive relationship that he felt he had had with his mother, he has dealt with his loss of father by becoming a woman (his mother) through emasculating himself, but gaining a man (his father) as a lover. This situation with all its attendant fears has forced him to give up all masculine identity.

He came into analysis five times a week. Mr D was a very young child when his father left home; he was left with his mother and an older brother. His mother became depressed; he felt that she turned to him at this time and he became an antidepressant factor in her life. She had also lost a sister when she was younger. He developed the idea around the age of 5 that he was in fact a woman and this grew until around the age of 18, so that he was convinced that he would have to undergo an operation to turn himself into a 'woman'. Thus he dealt with the loss of his father and the mentally absent mother by phantasising about turning himself into the primary object. This idea eventually developed until he was about to enact the crisis underlying the transsexual wish, that is, the cutting of and disposal of his penis – it becoming the cut-off unloved father. He imagined himself becoming the longed-for sexual phantasy of men who would want to come to him for sexual pleasure. So rather than losing anything, he had at once turned himself into the mother by becoming her in his phantasy. In this he could become a desirable figure for men, and through seducing them he could regain the father he had lost. The castrating father would be played by the surgeons who would cut off his penis, courtesy of the NHS. He was suicidal when he started treatment and adamant that if he was not allowed to have surgery he would enact this suicidal wish. Thus, in the transference, anything that I might have to say was instantly degraded and I had to subjugate my own thinking to his.

Two years later the following session occurred. The analytic work over this time had been very painful for him. He had used intellectual defences, destroying his knowledge of the need for love by making life into an examination, keeping at bay his pain and loneliness and depression over his absent father. As he changed there was a greater awareness of the life he got from his analysis. This had been accompanied by both a fear of losing me and a hatred of my limitations. He would often feel as if he has two analysts, a Friday one who helps him and a weekend one who is so preoccupied with his own life that he no longer matters at all. He then feels rescued on Monday by my returning. On a recent Monday he reported a dream: he had been aware of the death of his mother and there were very painful feelings and he felt that in the dream he was crying for his dead mother. He then found himself walking in some mountains away from it all; then terrifyingly he was on top of a very large dirty hole and the whole structure begins to shake and threatened to collapse under him. There is a man trying to save him. He takes a length of rope and throws it to him and he just manages to hold on to it before the hole seems to collapse under him, and he is saved. I said that he is aware that on the weekend he gets inside his analysis and kills it off; he then becomes terrified that he is going to be stuck inside a dead body of an analysis that will crumble all around him. He then feels relieved on returning to find that it and I are strong enough to survive his attacks. This led to an anxiety that it was his murderous thoughts that had driven away his father.

Ms P

In female homosexuality there is often a similar scenario. Ms P is a 38-year-old Italian woman who is homosexual and has had a monogamous relationship with a woman 8 years younger than herself for 15 years. She was 4 years old when her father died; mother never remarried and was felt by Ms P to make excessive demands on her; she eventually left home and emigrated to this country. She met her girlfriend here and soon became the dominant partner in the relationship. She works as a sheet metal worker in a factory and adopts most of the roles in the relationship that stereotypically would be associated with men. She is also very rigid and masculine in her mode of relating. It seems that she has dealt with the loss of her father by turning away from her need for him; she puts this into her mother who she then looks after in a fused claustrophobic relationship which later she recreates with her girlfriend. Her complaint about her girlfriend is that she will not allow her to lead her own life. She has no desire to be heterosexual but sought out a male analyst who is known to treat homosexuals. In the first session she described how, in comparison with women, she soon gets bored with men and her mind wanders off and she forgets them. It seems that she dealt with the loss of her father by becoming identified with the male role, projecting all her desperate wanting of a male partner (or father) into her female partner (or mother). She then phantasises that she has the capacity to deal with her own need of a male partner, projected into her lesbian partner.

This reversal and consequent projection of the depression and unhappiness is often quite bizarre; in fact the more extreme the anxiety, the more traumatised and disturbed the patient.

Another example of this is in paedophilia, where the younger the victim of child sexual abuse, the more psychotic is the underlying behaviour. The child becomes the 'container' of the adult's infantile self.

In the perversions we have a physical expression of severe pathological narcissism where the aim of the behaviour is to destroy any knowledge of the need for the other. All love is taken out of the object and attributed to something that stands for part of the self. The enactment is often an accurate expression of events or traumas in the subject's life which like a dream have to be enacted on others to enable the subject to feel relief from their own fears of annihilation. This is often at the level of total annihilation of the other as a separate person, so that they see in the recipient the split-off unwanted parts of the self. This is therefore a total expression of narcissism where the interest of survival of the self comes before everything else and the other is therefore only important as an adjunct to achieving this end.

References

Abramowitz A (1986). Psycho-social outcomes of sex re-assignment surgery. *Journal of Consulting and Clinical Psychology* 54: 183–9.

Blanchard D (1985). Gender dysphoria. *Journal of Consulting and Clinical Psychology* 1: 295–304.

Bollas C (1993). *Annual Edward Glover Lecture*. Portman Clinic.

Brown C (1990). *Transsexuality in Principles and Practice of Forensic Psychiatry*. London: Churchill Livingston.

Brenman E (1985). Cruelty and narrow-mindedness. *International Journal of Psycho-Analysis* 6: 273–81.

Freud S (1905). Three essays on the theory of sexuality. *The Complete Psychological Works of Sigmund Freud*, standard edition, vol. 7. London: Hogarth Press.

Halberstadt-Freud CH (1991). *Freud, Proust, Perversion and Love*. Amsterdam: Swets & Zeitlinger.

Heimann P (1952). Certain functions of introjection and projection in early infancy. In: M Klein, P Heimann, S Isaacs, J Riviere (Eds), *Developments in Psycho-analysis*. London: Masefield Press.

Khan M M R(1979). *Alienation in Perversions*. London: Hogarth Press. (Reprinted in 1993 by Karnac Books, London).

Limentani A (1979). *Transsexuality*. (Reprinted in *Between Freud and Klein* (1989). London: Free Association Press).

Morgan D (1995). *The Child as a Container for the Adult Infantile Self*, in press.

Rosenfeld H (1971). A clinical approach to the psychoanalytical theory of the life and death instincts: an investigation into the aggressive aspects of narcissism. *International Journal of Psycho-Analysis* 52: 169–78.

Sohn L (1985). Narcissistic organisation projective identification and the formation of the identificate. *International Journal of Psycho-Analysis* 66: 201–13.

Chapter 13
Addiction as a narcissistic defence: the importance of control over the object

LIZ GOOD

The subject of addiction has been relatively neglected in the analytic literature. Psychoanalytic theoreticians have traditionally regarded addiction primarily as a regressive phenomenon centred around the idea of fixation of libido in the oral phase of development. This regressive phenomenon involves the tendency in the addict towards 'acting-out' behaviour, not commensurate with a successful therapeutic alliance, so these patients have historically been considered unsuitable for analytical work. However, with the increased availability of drugs and the epidemic phenomenon of drug use and abuse, together with the success of many addicts in becoming completely drug free, psychotherapists are gaining greater insight into the psychic organisations within which addictions can take hold.

Addiction covers a wide diagnostic spectrum and tends to be a phenomenon that is understood diversely and subjectively by different clinicians. The working definition of addiction, adhered to for the purpose of this chapter, relates to patients who, through their own admission, have at times in their lives totally lost control of their chemical intake over a prolonged period of time, resulting in psychological and physical dependency on a chemical. Theoretically, when considering the specific psychopathology of addicts, there is a general consensus that addiction is a syndrome relating to psychoses, or psychosis-like conditions. Often the drug is seen as holding off an acute psychosis which would overwhelm the ego if the drug were withdrawn. The psychotic attempts to alter reality, whereas the addict aims to modify his own consciousness in order to avoid dysphoric affects. Therefore, in terms of formulating a theoretical diagnosis, broadly speaking these patients tend to be described as having borderline/narcissistic personality organisations.

The word narcissism comes from the Greek '*Narka*', to deaden. As Levin (1993, p. 40) states:

Both narcotics and (excessive) narcissism deaden, attenuate sensation and feeling. That says something interesting about addiction and its relationship to narcissism. The Greek route takes on its meaning of deadening from the name of Narcissus, the myth protagonist . . . a beautiful youth who becomes so entranced by his reflection in a pool of water that he remains frozen, gazing upon his own face until he perishes.

Some authors view narcissistic disorders as stemming from an intense vulnerability in the self and attempts at cohesion being repeatedly thwarted by unempathetic maternal responses. Others believe that narcissistic pathology results not from the disruption in the primary affectional bond between mother and infant, to which the mother contributes, but more from the envious and omnipotent attacks made by the infant upon the link between the mother and himself. It is Klein's view that the young infant is in a state of primary persecutory anxiety; therefore, all feelings of dependency upon someone elicit negative feelings. Analytical thinking has evolved concerning the aetiology, diagnosis and treatment of the narcissistic person. A great deal of this work concentrates on the crucial role of aggression in the aetiology of narcissism. Today narcissism is mainly seen as the result of developmental arrest. In an attempt to understand this difficult group of patients the following two views have both proved useful:

1. Narcissism as a defensive structure erected as a result of environmental failure
2. Narcissism as a defence against the internal hatred the infant has towards the object of its dependency.

Most addicts will pinpoint their addiction to the period of adolescence. Even though physical chemical dependency may not establish itself until much later in life, there is usually clear evidence and awareness in the individual of a psychological preoccupation, before the physical dependency manifesting itself. Drug addiction is but one form of expression of pathological symptomatology. Other expressions may find release in periodic psychotic episodes, compulsive actions, violent actions, eating disorders, psychosomatic disorders, etc.

The predisposition to drug addiction

Early adolescence is a time when excitation, tension, gratification and defensive issues relating to previous years, that is, during the psychosexual development of infancy and early childhood, return. This infantile admixture is responsible for the bizarreness and regressive character of adolescent behaviour. Adolescence could be considered the second edition of childhood. Blos (1962) reminds us that early adolescence involves the genuine process of separation from early object ties. The main feature of early adolescence resides in the decathexis of the incestuous love objects. Even though, by adolescence, the young person has achieved values and morals independent of the parental authority, nevertheless, during early adolescence, self-control threatens to break down and in extreme cases delinquency takes over. These delinquent actions may vary in degree of intensity, but usually are related to the search for a love object. These actions also offer escape from loneliness, isolation and depression which tends to accompany the cathectic shifts. Blos (1962, p. 76) states:

> Normally, acting-out is forestalled by a recourse to phantasy, to auto-eroticism, to ego alterations – for instance, a deflection of the object libido onto the self, which is to say, by a recourse to narcissism.

Adolescence is a time when narcissism is heightened and narcissistic defences could be interpreted as the adolescent's inability to give up the gratifying parent, on whom the child depends, as opposed to developing his own faculties. When such a child enters adolescence, he or she could find him- or herself totally unable to bear the pain of disillusionment. Or, alternatively, the process of separation may give rise to so much aggression and chaos that the child feels completely overwhelmed. I would postulate that it is at this point that an adolescent may well be vulnerable to the development of addiction, if drugs are being used or experimented with. If the adolescent is experiencing intense emotional upheaval, which leaves him or her feeling chaotic, aggressive and unable to cope, then the use of a drug may help to control these feelings and produce a sense of inner harmony. It could be argued that the drug symbolically represents the object that cannot be experienced as separate, and that the use of the drug means that the adolescent, in phantasy, gains control over the internal object (which is experienced as omnipotent before separation), as well as his or her emotional state. The need to control affects and preserve a narcissistic state is paramount. Therefore, addiction could be viewed as a narcissistic defence against primitive oral–sadistic feelings, which return during adolescence as the process of dependency and separation is negotiated. The implications of the returning infantile feelings, associated with the oral–sadistic state of development, overwhelm the adolescent and, if drugs are being used, they may take on special significance in the adolescent's inner world as a means of controlling these chaotic feelings.

Addiction as a narcissistic defence is paradoxical. Initially, drugs are used to contain destructive elements which threaten the individual's sense of integrity. The emphasis is on control of affects and, in phantasy, the primary object. In reality, addiction is the ultimate loss of control over the drug/object and it creates, in an exaggerated form, some of the painful affects it set out to avoid. For instance, after every 'hit', it is not long until depression, despair and panic set in about where the next fix will come from. The psychological torment of the impending loss represents such an existential nightmare that many recovering addicts report a dissolute experience which is indescribable and often the motivating factor behind many chronic drug abusers achieving abstinence from all mood-altering chemicals. In other words, the loss of the narcissistic gratification achieved by the drug produces such overwhelming pain that, in many cases, the depression brought about by abstinence is preferable to the persecution of active addiction. Therefore, some addicts grow out of their addictions by achieving an ability to tolerate, to some degree, depressive anxieties, as opposed to the paranoia/persecution associated with active addiction.

Let us return to the world of paradoxes that addiction forces us to recognise. For many addicts, active addiction does in fact act as a successful narcissistic defence for many years. Why, then, do some addicts abuse chemicals to such an extent that the defensive properties are destroyed and often the addict's life is in danger?

Klein singles out envy as one of the fundamental and primitive emotions. Envy arises in early infancy and is directed at the feeding breast. The love, warmth, care and food received by the infant could stir up opposite/paradoxical reactions: narcissistic gratification leading to love, hostility and envy at the awareness that the source of goodness lies outside the infant. Perhaps the narcissistic gratification achieved through addiction is destroyed by the addict, because drugs represent 'external objects' that are needed. Addicts cannot bear to feel dependent, because to depend means hatred, envy and intolerable frustrations.

The importance of omnipotent control versus separation

Some of the clinical observations/themes presented in this chapter emanate from many years working psychodynamically with a group of patients who have all been chronically addicted, but who have given up drugs for about 2 years before entering psychotherapy.

Fenichel (1945), when discussing addicts, informs us that patients who are ready to give up all object libido are necessarily people who have never estimated object-relationships very highly. He believed addicts to be fixated to a passive–narcissistic aim and to be interested solely in getting their gratification, never in satisfying their partners or, for that matter, in the specific personalities of their partners. Objects are nothing else for them but deliverers of supplies! I do not know that I would be as pessimistic as Fenichel. However, in my experience, for addicts, or recovering addicts, to survive and relate in the world of objects, there tends to be a 'need' for at least one area where total control (in phantasy) of the object can be reinforced and acted out. Many recovering addicts achieve high levels of recovery and develop areas of their lives that are progressive and successful. However, there tends to be a psychic compromise. They tolerate the frustrations emanating from the world of relationships only if there is an area (split off and hidden from everyone in their lives) where they re-enact the need for mastery over the object. Most drug addicts maintain adequate control over their addictions for many years, and it is only on rare occasions, or at the later/chronic stage of addiction, that they begin to lose control of the drug, and of their internal world. Paradoxically, abstinence from all drugs could be viewed as a satisfactory way of re-establishing control and the destructive/abusive aspects, in terms of drug/object relating, manifest themselves in other ways.

I intend to concentrate the rest of this chapter on describing three of the underlying clinical themes relating to the narcissistic need for omnipotent control over the 'other' and how this presents itself in the clinical work. I shall focus my attention on areas that continually manifest themselves when working with addicts, i.e. the fear of death, deception and prostitution.

Intense fear of death

My work with drug addicts demonstrates that separation is experienced as deadly. Often the thrust of adolescence hurls the young person into unwanted maturation, which is experienced as a frightening independence often associated with the recognition of death (suicide) as a resolution of the intense conflict. These patients fail to achieve the mourning required during the period of adolescence, because their fragile egos often become overwhelmed by the actual distress that they are suffering, together with the reawakening and heightened thanatophobia of infancy. They demonstrate a pervasive fear of change, because change brings with it the letting go of the familiar, and a moving on to . . . what? This developmental space is fraught with agonising anxiety which desiccates any hope of survival. Stern (1968) states that the fear of death is essentially the fear of repetition of mortal terror, experienced in the early biotraumatic states of object loss – involving the possibility of the ego's extinction. Drug addiction is an 'acting-out' of this overwhelming fear of death, as well as an omnipotent attempt at mastery over death. Every time the heroin addict injects him- or herself, he or she cannot be certain of what is actually in the concoction. Many intravenous heroin addicts recall instances of waking up with needles hanging out of their arms.

> One patient, I shall name Tom, had been abstinent from drugs for 3 years, but had begun to behave promiscuously. He was a 27-year-old homosexual man who suffered intense anxiety and tended to cope with his anxiety by frequent-

ing Hampstead Heath, picking up sexual partners, sometimes several in one evening, and indulging in unprotected sex. Tom was aware that he was behaving in a self-destructive manner, given that some of the partners he had sex with he suspected of being intravenous drug abusers. Shortly after entering therapy with me, Tom was diagnosed HIV positive. After the initial trauma of having to face the implications of this diagnosis, Tom became less anxious and began to work in his therapy. The change was quite remarkable. It became clear, in the therapy, that his anxiety, which related to paranoid/persecutory feelings about death, drastically reduced after he was diagnosed as HIV positive. It would appear that his death had now, in some way, come under his omnipotent control. Separation anxiety was experienced as living with the constant fear of death.

To bring about his own death, so to speak, seemed to produce a sense of mastery over separation/death. This patient achieved an ability to be free of intense anxiety in order to live what was left of his life with some relief from the persecutory anxiety that had 'ruined' his life.

Greenberg (1975) states that death is a state of eternal trauma. Previous traumatic situations have been survived, but from death there is no recovery – the outcome is fatal. The intense relief and pleasure associated with the ingestion of the drug resembles the mother–infant symbiosis which protects the infant from trauma/death. The gratification of libidinal needs through neutralising internal aggression wards off annihilation, and re-establishes the symbiosis as a defence against separation/death anxiety. Often these patients experience loss or separation as intense humiliation and degradation. In other words, loss feels like a persecutory and offensive attack on their integrity as human beings.

Addiction is paradoxical. It often brings about the very affects it seeks to prevent. Drug addicts do not always achieve mastery over death; many of them die. As mentioned above, separation is felt as a horrific experience, yet after every 'hit' the addict is faced with the possibility of this narcissistic state of energy wearing off, reducing him or her to psychic as well as physical despair. No sooner has one hit been secured when the anxiety about mastering the next has to be faced. However, while it lasts the drug does produce an inner harmony – the homeostasis that Grunberger (1989) describes – and many of these patients describe themselves as 'normal' only when they are intoxicated. Frequently cocaine addicts experience such heightened arousal that the sexual orgasm is reduced to a second-rate experience. Rado (1926) believes that the 'alimentary orgasm' – which is first experienced by the infant at the breast – is revived in drug addiction, and sexual excitation belonging to phantasies of the Oedipal situation is discharged, not by means of onanism but through the alimentary orgasm. He suggests that in chronic drug addiction the whole personality represents an autoerotic (narcissistic) pleasure apparatus. Therefore, heroin addicts especially can find a harmony and peace with themselves and life, and a drug-free existence can feel like a terrible deprivation. Most of us strive for some sort of narcissistic gratification through our creativity, work, children, etc. Sometimes we achieve recognition, but mostly we have to be content with being ordinary and reduced to the striving. However, with addiction, people have crossed the borderline of normality and often for many years have managed to be narcissistically gratified, as long as the drug was available. This chapter asks the question of whether or not it is possible, having achieved some control over a narcissistic state, that one can ever give it up and return to the world of reality where loss and disillusionment are common place.

Deception and secret worlds

The 'art' of deception – a perverse statement perhaps, yet representing some truth as there is clearly a great deal of creative energy, albeit destructively aimed, prevalent in addicts. Often these patients have managed to hide their addiction from family, friends, colleagues and spouses for many years. They have cheated, robbed, lied and manipulated in an attempt to hide their secret worlds. Winnicott's theory of the 'false self' (1960) is helpful in understanding some of the unconscious processes that underlie the secrecy and deception relating to the 'underworld' that addicts are drawn to.

Often these patients enter therapy, conscious of their attempts to deceive the therapist. Why do they come to therapy? Perhaps it is, as Winnicott states, 'the false self brings the true self to therapy'. However, I think that this brings us back to the world of paradoxes/ambivalence/splitting. Basically, a part of them wants a meaningful experience, but another part, a more malignant part, does not want to enter an honest process of relating to another as this would mean a lack of control of the other. Deception is a defensive manoeuvre to avoid being related to, or found in, the therapeutic experience. Often recovering addicts can restore their lives and more or less present as fairly normal human beings. However, there tends to be secret worlds where their narcissism is indulged and contained. This secret world is often hidden from everyone including the therapist. The secret world may be an extramarital affair, the use of pornography and eating disorders, such as bulimia or anorexia nervosa. These areas are closely guarded and may take several years to enter the consulting room.

Fairbairn (1952) reminds us that frustration gives rise to aggression, which is an infantile reaction to deprivation and frustration in the libidinal relationship, and, in particular, to the trauma of separation from the primary object. Therefore, ambivalence is a reaction to deprivation and frustration. According to Fairbairn, to be able to control an un-satisfying object, the infant employs a defensive process, i.e. internalisation, to remove it from the outer world (where it eludes his control) to the inner world (where the object can be controlled). By controlling the object of his desire, the child limits the risk of disappointment and rejection by his mother.

Fairbairn described the 'over-exciting' and 'over-frustrating' (ambivalent) aspects of the internalised object and how they become unacceptable to the original ego. Therefore, splitting of the object gives rise to the 'exciting' object and the 'rejecting' object. The libidinal self is attached to the exciting object and the anti-libidinal self is attached to the rejecting object, or 'internal saboteur'. The secret world of the addict allows him to re-find, in an attempt to work through the pain of the seductive/frustrating object, which affords him some leeway in reality in terms of protection of the good object/mother/therapist who does not totally satisfy. Let me give an example of the secret world of Colin.

Soon after Colin gave up drugs, he met a young woman and decided to marry. When they announced their decision they were both basking in their love for each other. However, as she became preoccupied with 'her' wedding plans, as this was to be a lavish affair, he became more and more withdrawn. He took no interest in the wedding. Any attempt to explore his withdrawn, depressed state resulted in him idolising his wife-to-be and reassuring himself that all was well. He then started an affair (with an extremely destructive, young, female addict). The affair lasted until just before his wedding when his fiancée found out. During this time, he was unreachable by me. Any attempts at interpretation were lost. He was maniacally defended against any feelings towards his fiancée or me and seemed intoxicated with the excitement and terror attached to his affair. After his affair was discovered, he ended the relationship and went through with his marriage. He was initially remorseful, but quickly recovered. However, he continued the affair after he got married on a secret and extremely sporadic basis. He deceived his wife (and myself) by omission for many months. As we explored his deviousness within the therapy, he admitted that he had continued the affair and that he had never been faithful to any woman. He found his wife disappointing in many ways – she was not intelligent enough, she was too 'straight', etc. He could not bear the disappointment and hatred he felt, without having a 'secret' which would excite him, even though this excitement was dangerous. The deception was his way of controlling his overwhelming feelings of hatred, that his wife, like his mother, and like me, were unable to satisfy all of his needs. He was afraid that his aggression would destroy the good things that he valued, i.e. his wife and his therapy. He was even more afraid of investing his love in his marriage, or his therapy, for fear of losing himself in overwhelming despair, which he sensed existed within him.

A couple of years later, his wife became pregnant and at 8 months into her pregnancy she found out that he was still having an affair. The affair escalated as soon as he discovered that his wife was pregnant. It appeared that his marriage was acceptable to him only when narcissistically gratified. Clearly he could not tolerate not being the centre of attention. His destructive attacks manifested themselves at times when his wife's narcissism was heightened and she had less energy available for him. He felt left out when she was planning 'her' wedding and when she was pregnant with 'her' baby. He could not tolerate not being the special one. Unconsciously, I think this reminded him of his alcoholic mother who at times was boozily over-indulgent but at other times was remote, withdrawn and preoccupied with her own problems.

The secret world (and perverse addictive object choice) could be viewed as a libidinal attempt to restore the lost unity of the self. However, with addicts, there is such a level of aggression/destruction that these attempts at understanding could also have suicidal/homicidal elements to them. Therefore, deception is often conscious, but the need for the 'secret world' is unconscious, and it is about a pervasive need to maintain control over internal objects. Fairbairn throws some light on the need for 'secrets' when he highlights the narcissistic inflation of the ego arising out of secret possession of, and identification with, internalised libidinal objects. Fairbairn (1952, p. 22) draws our attention to the inner necessity for secrecy as being 'partly determined by guilt over the possession of internalised objects which are in a sense "stolen", but it is also in no small measure determined by fear of the loss of internalised objects which appear infinitely precious (even as precious as life itself) and the internalisation of which is a measure of their importance and the extent of dependence upon them'.

The deceptive secret world that addicts are used to is often consciously hidden, although the need for this world remains unconscious and compulsively entered into as a means of control over internal objects at times of heightened psychological crisis associated with the experience of loss, deprivation or frustration. As far as their real needs have not been acknowledged, but have been replaced by excitement, the destructive part of the personality has seized control and the narcissistic organisation has resurfaced.

Prostitution and control

I would like to stress a third clinical theme which relates to the importance of prostitution in the everyday life of addicts and recovering addicts. Elements of prostitution exist in both male and female addicts. When addicts are physically addicted many of them report histories of having prostituted themselves in order to acquire money for drugs. However, when you consider the whole concept of addiction, i.e. the addict (client) obtains the drug by visiting the 'dealer' (prostitute), whereby he pays for the drug (object) at will. Both dealer and addict, or prostitute and client, see this dynamic as mutually fulfilling needs without the emotional complications of having to relate in a meaningful way. Interestingly, this phenomenon continues to be re-enacted by many recovering addicts who no longer have the excuse that they need the money for drugs. Glover (1943) states that the sexual life of both client and prostitute contains a marked component of sadism, either manifest or latent, whose injurious consequences indicate an unconscious masochistic component in which mutual depreciation is the rule. According to Welldon (1988, p. 114):

In prostitution both parties are seeking control . . . I believe that both parties are involved in some compromise whereby the sexual mother is being taken over by the strict mother, provider of bodily ministrations. The woman is clearly in charge of the initial contact and, in some cases, of the outcome too. However, the man shares the same expectation. In his view, since he pays he is in charge, and he knows exactly what the outcome will be. He pays for the illusion that he won't be taken over by an all-invading mother, and therefore he feels safe.

The use of a prostitute is a substitute for, and tends to ward off, aggression and sadism towards the object. Many of these patients attempt to use the therapist in the same way as they would a prostitute.

John came to therapy and would often miss sessions. As we explored his behaviour it became clear that his attitude was that I should put up with whatever he did – after all he was paying me. I was experienced as someone who provided a service and took money for that service, therefore he considered it his right to treat me in whatever manner pleased him. I interpreted that he treated me in the same way as the prostitutes he visited; so as not to deal with me as a real person, he became extremely angry and for several months he 'acted out' this rage by visiting prostitutes either on the way to sessions or after his sessions with me. Before he could be able accept this interpretation and relate to me as a real person, I was experienced in the transference as a tyrannical mother who forced him to do things (such as come to his sessions) against his will. He took his revenge on me out on the prostitutes he visited, who were forced to do 'his will'.

Other patients come to their sessions and believe that, because they pay for 'professional services', then they have a right to demand that the therapist should perform by relieving their symptoms. The idea of working on their difficulties is anathema to them, and again, as reality dawns, rage emerges at the 'lack of service' provided.

Sexuality becomes confused with the need for control of the other. Control is the opposite of impotence and engulfment, which is feared by many of these patients. What prostitution and drug addiction have in common is that there is a need to create a pre-Oedipal perverse dyadic relationship (in phantasy) which is illegal and leaves the participants constantly persecuted by the 'other' (i.e. the law, the spouse, the therapist). Again in prostitution, as in addiction, there is always an element of danger, which could be viewed as a manic defence, covering up depression and emptiness and where the lethal component of narcissism is acted out.

Often these patients need to delude themselves that they are in total control of the therapy, and this situation, in my opinion, should not be interpreted too early. As, in the process of addiction, the addict soon realises that the drug being used is not under his or her control, a similar process takes place in the therapy, except it is hoped that this experience can be a reparative one whereby difficult feelings can be contained and worked through so that the patient can develop some insight into his or her extremely vulnerable inner world.

References

Blos P (1962). *On Adolescence, A Psychoanalytic Interpretation*. New York: Free Press.

Fairbairn WRD (1952). *Psychoanalytic Studies of the Personality*. London: Routledge & Keegan Paul.

Fenichel O (1945). *The Psychoanalytic Theory of Neurosis*. New York: Norton.

Glover E (1943).The psychopathology of prostitution. *Edward Glover Lecture*, pp. 1–66. Institute of Study and Treatment of Delinquency.

Greenberg HR (1975). The widening gyre: transformations of the omnipotent quest during adolescence. *International Review of Psycho-Analysis* 2: 231.

Grunberger B (1989). *New Essays on Narcissism*. London: Free Association Books.

Levin DL (1993). *Slings and Arrows. Narcissistic Injury and Its Treatment*. New Jersey: Jason Aaron.

Rado S (1926). The psychic effects of intoxification: attempts at a psycho-analytic theory of drug addiction. *International Journal of Psycho-Analysis* 7.

Stern M (1968). Fear of death and neurosis. *International American Psycho-Analytic Association* 16: 3–31.

Welldon EV (1988). *Mother, Madonna, Whore*. New York: Guilford Press.

Winnicott DW (1960). Ego distortions in terms of true and false self. In: *The Maturational Processes and the Facilitating Environment*. London: Karnac Books and Institute of Psycho-Analysis.

Index